Collins · *do brilliantly!*

D1427416

2005TestPractice

KS3 Shakespeare
Macbeth

Test practice at its **best**

■ **Mike Gould**

■ **Series Editor: Jayne de Courcy**

William Collins' dream of knowledge for all began with the publication of his first book in 1819.
A self-educated mill worker, he not only enriched millions of lives, but also founded a flourishing publishing house.
Today, staying true to this spirit, Collins books are packed with inspiration, innovation and practical expertise.
They place you at the centre of a world of possibility and give you exactly what you need to explore it.

Collins. Do more.

Published by Collins
An imprint of HarperCollins*Publishers*
77–85 Fulham Palace Road
Hammersmith
London
W6 8JB

Browse the complete Collins catalogue at
www.collinseducation.com

10 9 8 7 6 5 4 3 2 1

ISBN 0 00 719410 2

Mike Gould asserts the moral right to be identified as the author of this work.

British Library Cataloguing in Publication Data
A Catalogue record for this publication is available from the British Library

Edited by Joanne Hunt
Illustrated by Harriet Buckley, Fliss Cary, Sarah Wimperis
Production by Katie Butler
Book design by Bob Vickers
Printed and bound by Printing Express, Hong Kong

Acknowledgements
Cambridge University Press for extracts from *Macbeth* by William Shakespeare, edited by A R Braunmuller,
The New Cambridge Shakespeare Series, 1997 © Cambridge University Press, reproduced with permission.

Photographs
The Author and Publishers are grateful to the following for permission to reproduce photographs:
Historical Picture Archive/CORBIS (p8 top); Bettmann/CORBIS (p8 centre); Bettmann/CORBIS (p9);
Robbie Jack/CORBIS (p10); Robbie Jack/CORBIS (p13); Donald Cooper/Photostage (p18);
Donald Cooper/Photostage (p21); Donald Cooper/Photostage (p24); Donald Cooper/Photostage (p33);
Joe Cocks Studio Collection Copyright Shakespeare Birthplace Trust (p37); Donald Cooper/Photostage (p38);
Robbie Jack/CORBIS (p48); Reg Wilson © RSC (p53).

You might also like to visit:
www.harpercollins.co.uk
The book lover's website

Contents

How this book will help you

Test Practice KS3 Shakespeare: Macbeth has been designed to help you gain a high level in the Shakespeare Paper of your English National Test. Here is how:

1. It provides a **detailed commentary on *Macbeth*** covering all the areas you need to know about: plot, characters, themes and language.

2. It prepares you for the **Shakespeare Paper** by giving you expert guidance on the **techniques and skills** you need in order to answer questions well.

3. It gives you a **complete practice paper** based on the **set scenes for 2005** as well as **level indicators** and **sample answers**.

Section 1 UNDERSTANDING THE PLAY

- **Unit 1** provides a **background** to *Macbeth*, focussing on interesting facts about the play, and an introduction to life in Shakespeare's times.

- **Unit 2** consists of a **scene–by–scene commentary** on the play. The plot analysis explains clearly *what* happens, *when* it happens – and *why*. Analysis is deepened with colour-coded references to **themes** which are examined in greater detail in **Unit 4**.

- **Unit 3** looks at **character**, analysing the behaviour and motives of each of the main characters in turn. There are quotations and evidence to back up the ideas.

- **Unit 4** looks at **key themes**, expanding on the colour-coded analysis in **Unit 2**.

- **Unit 5** examines key aspects of Shakespeare's use of **language** in *Macbeth*, looking at *what* is said, *how* it is said and the *effect* this has on the audience.

Section 2 HOW TO ANSWER TEST QUESTIONS

This section covers the **key skills and techniques** you need in order to do your best in the Shakespeare Paper. It tackles the most common problem areas for students in the Test and provides you with the techniques to answer questions well.

Each of the units in **Sections 1 and 2** have the following:

QUICK CHECK

Short questions which test your understanding.

do brilliantly!

Essential hints on how to get the **TOP LEVELS** in your Test and **examples** of answers that score a high level.

Section 2 also provides:

TIP

Simple, easy-to-remember advice.

Section 3 PRACTICE PAPER

This section gives you the chance to do **two practice questions** on your set scenes from the play. It also provides:

- detailed **level indicators** showing what Test markers are looking for when awarding marks;

- **sample answers** from students **at different levels** so you can compare your work with theirs and **practise improving your answer** in order to raise the grade.

What you need to know about the Shakespeare Paper

This book is all about preparing you to write a good answer on *Macbeth* in the Shakespeare Paper. In order to prepare effectively, you need to know what is involved and be clear about what you are working towards. **Section 3** gives you practice at answering questions, but you need to keep your mind on the Test from the start of this book.

So, here's a **summary of what you are required to do in the Test**:

● You will be given **ONE question** based on your study of *Macbeth*.
● You will need to spend **45 minutes** answering it.

The question will be based on the **following scenes for 2005**:

> **Act 3 Scene 1 (line 75 to the end of the scene):**
> *'Was it not yesterday we spoke together?'*
>   to
> *'If it find heaven, must find it out tonight.'*
>   and
>
> **Act 3 Scene 2 (whole scene):**
> *'Is Banquo gone from court?'*
>   to
> *'So prithee, go with me.'*
>   and
>
> **Act 3 Scene 4 (whole scene):**
> *'You know your own degrees, sit down;'*
>   to
> *'We are yet but young in deed.'*

In the actual Test, **shorter extracts** from **two of these scenes** will be included on your Shakespeare Paper.

You should **base your answers on the extracts you are given in the Test**.

Finally, some extra advice

Try to see a performance of *Macbeth* (either on stage or on film). Although you are working towards a Test, **you can still enjoy the play**. After all, it has a great story, memorable characters, and powerful language.

Most importantly of all, imagine the play in performance as you study it and use this book. Don't forget that Shakespeare was himself an actor and wrote his plays for performance. Remember that there is an audience if there is a performance!

> If you use this book to help you gain a thorough understanding of *Macbeth* and how to answer Test questions on it, there is no doubt that you will *do brilliantly*!

Brush up your Shakespeare!

Macbeth was first performed to audiences in 1606 and, before you started studying the play, you had probably already heard of it. After all, *Macbeth* is still one of Shakespeare's most famous and most performed plays.

But, did you know...?

The Real Macbeth

- Macbeth was a *real* king. He became ruler in 1040 after the death of Duncan, who was seen as a rather weak and unpopular ruler. No one knows whether the real Macbeth killed him to claim the throne, but we do know that Scotland at that time was full of murderous clans (tribes) all competing for power. Indeed, Macbeth's own father was murdered by his cousins.

- During Macbeth's 17-year reign, Scotland was a relatively stable and peaceful country as the north and south were united. However, Macbeth was killed in 1057 by the army of Duncan's son, Malcolm. The soldiers of the English king, Edward the Confessor, supported Malcolm's army.

THE CURSE OF 'THAT PLAY'

- There have been quite a few serious accidents and strange deaths connected with the performance of *Macbeth*. As a result, many actors and actresses think it is bad luck to say the name of the play and instead call it 'the Scottish play'.

- During what was possibly the first ever performance of *Macbeth* on August 7th 1606, the actor playing Lady Macbeth – a boy named Hal Berridge – died mysteriously backstage.

A play about sleep?

- *Macbeth* is about murder, kingship, ambition and power, but it is also about **sleep**.

- There are over 30 references to sleep in the play! Have a look through the play and see how many of these references you can find. Who talks of sleep? What happens to several of the characters whilst they sleep?

The Third Man... or Woman

In the play, we see Macbeth hire *two* murderers to kill Banquo. However, when the murder takes place a mysterious, unnamed *third* murderer appears. This is also not expected by the two other murderers.

The third murderer knows a lot about Banquo's movements – he, or she, knows at what time Banquo and his son, Fleance, will be where, and it is he – or she – who recognises Banquo. Is the third murderer Macbeth, in disguise – or someone else? If it is someone else, who could it be?

It is **ambiguous**, which means there is no way we can 'know' for sure.

Directors' interpretations

- It is important to remember that Shakespeare wrote his plays *for performance* and that different directors will choose to stage and interpret the play in their own way. The **text** remains the same, but the **staging** will vary according to each director.

- An example of this is Ken Hughes' 1955 film version of the play, called *Joe Macbeth*. Hughes gives the play a modern treatment – he makes Macbeth a gangster involved with organised crime. In it, the 'hero' visits a fortune-teller, not three witches, and the murders are committed by machine guns in restaurants.

An opera?

- Many people have tried to 'improve' *Macbeth*, by adapting the play. For example, in 1672, Sir William Davenant turned the play into a type of opera which included many songs and dances.

- Later, in the 18th century, the actor David Garrick added a long speech for the dying Macbeth.

- Even now, although the play is generally performed as it was in the 'original', there are disputes over certain scenes and who wrote them. One such scene is Act 3 Scene 5.

FACT AND FICTION

- Shakespeare, like many other writers, used the historian Raphael Holinshed's *Chronicles* as sources for the plots of many of his earlier plays. He used Holinshed again to find information about Macbeth when writing 'The Scottish Play'. As with Shakespeare's other plays which are based on real figures, he altered the original version in order to create his own, individual work.

- In Shakespeare's version of *Macbeth*, Banquo becomes Macbeth's enemy and Macbeth arranges his murder. However, in Holinshed's work Banquo is Macbeth's partner in the king's murder!

Oi! What are you doing here, Banquo? You're supposed to be the good guy!

Shakespeare also invented Lady Macbeth's suicide and her sleepwalking, plus the ghost of Banquo... amongst other things!

Is it a ghost?

Audiences in Shakespeare's day liked having a ghost in a play – someone who could physically appear on stage and speak. But in *Macbeth*, Banquo's ghost is a silent ghost which must have disappointed some Elizabethan theatre-goers. Today, many modern productions give a different interpretation and make him a figment of Macbeth's imagination. It is interesting to note that both appearances of Banquo's ghost happen just after Macbeth has referred to him.

So when is a ghost not a ghost? In Act 4 Scene 1, Banquo appears again, this time with the three 'apparitions'. They speak to Macbeth – but are they 'ghosts'? In the play they seem to have been conjured up by the Witches, but could this be Macbeth's imagination again?

Life in Shakespeare's times

> I know that Shakespeare was alive a long time ago, but do I really need to know what life was like in his day?

To enjoy the play, you don't. But if you really want to understand it, it does help if you know a little about the history.

Life in Shakespeare's time was very different to life in the 21st century. For example, you may wonder why Shakespeare was so obsessed with kings and wars. Well... William Shakespeare's baptism was recorded in **1564** and he died in **1616**. He lived through the reigns of two English monarchs. The first was **Elizabeth 1**, who reigned from **1558–1603**. Her reign was one of **great achievements** in the arts, exploration and scientific discovery.

Adventurers, such as **Sir Walter Raleigh**, sailed to distant lands, and brought back news of the places they visited and the people who lived in them. This was really exciting for Shakespeare and his contemporaries.

However, this golden age was also a time of **civil unrest**. Shakespeare and the actors in his company would have been very aware of the political situation that faced their monarch. They would have noted the **lack of an heir** to the throne and the **continuing disputes** over **Elizabeth's 'right'** to be **Queen**.

There were many plots against Queen Elizabeth I, and Shakespeare would have been aware of events such as the **Essex rebellion** (when the Earl of Essex attempted a raid on the Queen and London and was later executed for treason), and the **execution of rival Mary Queen of Scots** for plotting against the Queen.

> Who was the second monarch? After all, Elizabeth I died in 1603 and Shakespeare didn't die until 1616.

The second monarch was **James 1**, who lived from **1603–1625**. It was James who granted Shakespeare's acting company a royal licence, and made them **'King's Men'**.

The arts continued to develop. Many **new theatres** were built during this period and **literature flourished**. Some people say that Shakespeare wrote *Macbeth* to please King James I.

The original Globe Theatre, London

James' reign, like Elizabeth's before him, was also threatened by rebellion. James felt this threat at the very beginning of his reign, with the **Gunpowder Plot of 1605**. This was when **Guy Fawkes** and his fellow conspirators, tried to **blow up Parliament**.

James I would have enjoyed a play that depicted the ruin of a man who plotted against his King. Also, *Macbeth* is a play that deals with the **supernatural** and it was well known that James had an interest in this side of life.

Why is there so much about witches and witchcraft in *Macbeth*?

In Shakespeare's day the **supernatural** and **witchcraft** were serious matters. Educated people would have been aware of **the three Fates of Greek mythology**. These Fates (or 'Fatal Sisters') were believed to control the destiny (the fate) of all men and women. The three Witches in *Macbeth*, are often referred to as the 'weird sisters'.

So people believed in witchcraft?

Most people in Shakespeare's day believed in witches, including King James 1, who published a book called *Demonology*.

Many people were exposed as being witches and **burnt alive or hanged**. This was often a convenient way of blaming individuals when terrible things occurred for which there was no obvious explanation. Witches were mostly women, or people with what we might now call mental problems.

But weren't most of the population Christians?

Yes. People in Shakespeare's day were almost all Christian. They believed in the reality of Heaven and Hell, and would often see cruel events (such as the death of children, or bad luck) as punishment for their sins.

Today we have the benefit of a lot of scientific knowledge discovered since Shakespearean times. However, in those days, many everyday events and phenomena were put down to **supernatural forces**. As a result, people considered many aspects of life as magical or evil, whereas today, we would find rational explanations.

Stick to the scenes!

do brilliantly!

Although much of the information here is interesting, **do not** fall back on writing about Shakespeare, or his times, in the Test when you don't have much to say about the key scenes!

Markers will see right through you if you put:

Shakespeare was a great writer who knew King James really well, especially because Macbeth was possibly written for him and it was about lots of things the king was interested in...

Stick to the scenes you are studying! Outside information is only useful if it enables you to say something directly relevant about the character, language or themes. For example, if commenting on Macbeth's character, you could say...

Macbeth's fear of 'stones...(that)...have been known to move and trees to speak...' in Act 3 Scene 4, would have had even more power in Shakespeare's day, in front of a god-fearing, superstitious audience. It's no wonder Macbeth is shaken by seeing Banquo's ghost.

QUICK CHECK

1 Why do actors often not mention the play by its name?

2 What was the real Macbeth like?

3 What two monarchs reigned while Shakespeare was alive?

4 Where did Shakespeare get his story from?

5 Who - from myth and legend - might the three Witches have been based on?

6 How do we know that King James I was interested in the supernatural?

2 The plot: scene by scene

Act 1: Scenes 1 to 7

> Fair is foul, and foul is fair,
> Hover through the fog and
> filthy air.

Scene 1   The Witches meet

Three unnamed Witches appear in a deserted and wild place. They decide that they will meet Macbeth once the battle has finished. The scene ends with the Witches chanting what sounds like a spell.

Commentary

- Scene 1 **establishes the idea** that there are supernatural forces at work that are beyond the control of the characters.
- It sets the **atmosphere** of the play and the nature of the events to come.
- A **battle** is mentioned. It is clear the Witches **know the outcome**, as they know it will be finished *'ere the set of sun'* (before sunset).
- The **main character**, Macbeth, is mentioned, making us think: *why* do the Witches wish to meet him?

Themes

Appearance and reality: The words *'Fair is foul, and foul is fair…'* provide an omen for Macbeth's murderous behaviour and that what is 'seen' is not always to be trusted.

The supernatural: The only characters in this scene are Witches. They refer to creatures typically associated with Witches – Graymalkin (a cat) and Paddock (a toad). This suggests conjuring and spells.

Scene 2   Two battles are reported to King Duncan

We meet King Duncan as he is given news from the battlefield, where his forces are fighting rebels (which include the King of Norway).

Firstly, a wounded soldier (a 'captain') tells of two battles and reports that, in the first, Macbeth bravely killed a rebel called Macdonwald and speaks about the brave actions of Macbeth and another man, Banquo. Then Ross, one of the Scottish noblemen, reports the defeat of the Thane of Cawdor, a traitor who has rebelled against the King.

The King orders Cawdor's execution. Then he tells Ross to inform Macbeth that he will now be given the title Thane of Cawdor.

Commentary

- Macbeth's **apparent loyalty** and war-like spirit are established.
- Scene 2 introduces **Duncan, the King**, who Macbeth will murder, and **Banquo** – his close 'friend'.
- The **violent and graphic language** sets the tone for the play (*'reeking wounds'*, *'brandished steel'* are just two descriptions).
- We (the audience) learn that Macbeth is to become **Thane of Cawdor**.

Themes

Appearance and reality: The Thane of Cawdor is a traitor, but was once seen as loyal. Macbeth is now seen as loyal, but will become a traitor.

Ambition: The battles were for control of Scotland – Macbeth's reward is a promotion to Thane of Cawdor.

> All hail, Macbeth, that shalt be king hereafter.

Scene 3 The Witches meet Macbeth and Banquo

The three Witches await the arrival of Macbeth and Banquo. They talk about evil acts they have committed (e.g. '*killing swine*').

Macbeth and Banquo arrive, on their way back from the battle. The Witches speak to them and tell their prophecies:

- Macbeth will become **Thane of Cawdor**
- Macbeth will become **King**
- Banquo will be **father to future kings**.

The Witches then disappear.

The two lords, Ross and Angus, arrive and announce that Macbeth has been given the title 'Thane of Cawdor'. Macbeth is shocked by the news. The first prophecy has been proved correct!

Themes

The supernatural: The Witches appear, prophesise, and vanish magically.

Evil: Banquo is concerned about the '*instruments of darkness*' (meaning evil things/beings).

Ambition: The seeds of it are sown in Macbeth's mind.

Commentary

- The first **prophecy** is given – Macbeth to be Thane of Cawdor – and then fulfilled, which adds to the supernatural element, and sets up the Witches as a powerful force.
- Macbeth shows the first signs of his **murderous intentions**. (He says that he might '*yield to that suggestion*' – the suggestion in his mind that he might kill the king.)
- Macbeth also knows that **Banquo's children** could become kings.
- There is **dramatic irony** here. We know, before Macbeth does, that he is to be proclaimed Thane of Cawdor – and then he is!

Scene 4 Duncan greets Macbeth

This scene takes place at the Royal Palace where King Duncan is told about the death of the traitor, Cawdor. Then Macbeth and Banquo arrive and the King welcomes them warmly.

Duncan gives his son, Malcolm, the title, 'The Prince of Cumberland' and names him as his heir. This means Malcolm will be king if Duncan dies.

Duncan announces he will come to stay at Macbeth's castle. In his soliloquy to the audience, Macbeth starts to plot the king's downfall. Macbeth is unhappy that Malcolm has been made the heir.

Commentary

- Macbeth decides he **must hide his true intentions** (he says '*Stars, hide your fires, / Let not light see my black and deep desires...*').
- The audience sees Duncan as a victim, as we see him in a vulnerable position. We have all the information; Duncan has none.

Themes

Appearance and reality: Duncan is unaware of Macbeth's real feelings – he treats him warmly calling him '*worthiest cousin*'.
The old Thane of Cawdor was someone for whom the King had '*an absolute trust*'. Yet this man betrayed him.
Duncan reveals that he does not find it simple to judge the worth of a man: '*There's no art / To find the mind's construction in the face.*'.

Scene 5 Lady Macbeth reads the letter

At Macbeth's castle, Lady Macbeth reads a letter from her husband in which Macbeth tells her of the prophecies. She immediately starts plotting the King's death, but is worried that Macbeth may not be ruthless enough to do what is needed. A servant then appears and tells her that the King is going to be staying at their castle for one night.

Lady Macbeth calls on evil spirits ('*Come you spirits...*') to remove any sympathy from her. After greeting Macbeth she reveals her plan, warning him to hide his thoughts in public and exits after telling him to leave it all up to her.

Commentary

- **Lady Macbeth takes control**, sweeping Macbeth along and ignoring his attempt to regain some control ('*We will speak further*'), stating '*Leave all the rest to me*'.

- We see **how far Lady Macbeth is prepared to go** to get what she wants.

Themes

Evil: Lady Macbeth calls on evil 'spirits' to fill her with '*direst cruelty*', and to the '*murd'ring ministers*' to remove her woman's milk and make it poisonous.

Appearance and reality: Lady Macbeth warns her husband that he must appear welcoming to Duncan, and '*look like th' innocent flower, / But be the serpent under 't*'.

Ambition: It is Lady Macbeth's own ambition that is the driving force at this stage.

Scene 6 Duncan's arrival at Macbeth's castle

King Duncan and his court arrive at Macbeth's castle. Duncan speaks to Banquo of the pleasant surroundings, stating the '*air nimbly and sweetly recommends itself*'.

Lady Macbeth appears to welcome Duncan into the castle. She speaks of the loyalty and service due to the King for how he has honoured them.

Commentary

- We see **dramatic irony** here again. The audience knows what is to come. Duncan and Banquo do not.

- We witness **Duncan's trust** as he says '*Give me your hand; / Conduct me to mine host...*'

- This scene **contrasts with Act 2 Scene 4** when the Old Man and Ross stand outside the castle and describe the terrible night of the murder.

Themes

Appearance and reality: Because we know the truth about what the Macbeths are planning, we realise how wrong Banquo and Duncan are to see the castle and Lady Macbeth as welcoming. Banquo even compares the air to '*heaven's breath*'!

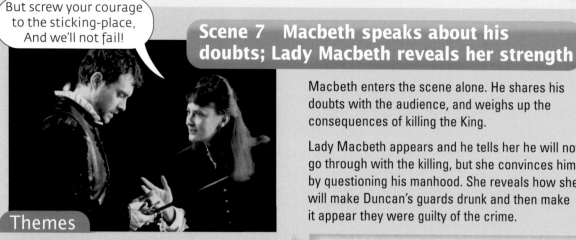

> But screw your courage to the sticking-place, And we'll not fail!

Scene 7   Macbeth speaks about his doubts; Lady Macbeth reveals her strength

Macbeth enters the scene alone. He shares his doubts with the audience, and weighs up the consequences of killing the King.

Lady Macbeth appears and he tells her he will not go through with the killing, but she convinces him by questioning his manhood. She reveals how she will make Duncan's guards drunk and then make it appear they were guilty of the crime.

Themes

Ambition: Macbeth recognises that he has no real desire to act against the King, but that ambition alone drives him. '*I have… only vaulting ambition…*'

Evil: Macbeth imagines that Duncan's virtues '*will plead like angels*', so to kill him will seem like an offence against God. Lady Macbeth, in contrast, says that she would have '*dashed the brains out*' of her own baby to fulfil her ambitions.

Appearance and reality: Macbeth closes the scene by talking of hiding the truth, and presenting a false face: '*False face must hide what the false heart doth know*'.

Commentary

- Macbeth, as host and subject, **airs his doubts** saying how the King is there '*in double trust…*'.
- Macbeth is **at first firm** '*We will proceed no further in this business.*'.
- Lady Macbeth **questions his manhood**.
- Yet Macbeth is **still hesitant**: '*If we should fail?*'
- After more encouragement, Macbeth **concedes**: '*I am settled*' (this shows Lady Macbeth's power and influence over her husband – or how easily he allows himself to be convinced).

QUICK CHECK

1. Who appear while the battle is on and agree to meet Macbeth once it is over? (Act 1 Scene 1)
2. Two different people report on Macbeth's bravery. Who are they? (Act 1 Scene 2)
3. What title does Duncan order should be given to Macbeth? (Act 1 Scene 2)
4. The Witches say Macbeth will be King. What do they promise to Banquo? (Act 1 Scene 3)
5. Who is named heir to the throne? (Act 1 Scene 4)
6. How should Macbeth behave, according to Lady Macbeth in Act 1 Scene 5?
7. What impression does Duncan get of Macbeth's castle when he arrives? (Act 1 Scene 6)
8. How does Lady Macbeth behave towards Duncan when he arrives? (Act 1 Scene 6)
9. How do we know that Macbeth is uncertain about whether to go through with the murder in Act 1 Scene 7?
10. How does Lady Macbeth persuade him?

Collect different pieces of evidence together

do brilliantly !

To **gain higher Test levels**, it is important that you do not look at just one piece of evidence. For example, if you were arguing that it is Macbeth who is the driving force behind the murders, you could mention that he:

- has the *initial* idea (Act 1 Scene 3)
- writes the letter to Lady Macbeth revealing his thoughts (Act 1 Scene 5)
- has his doubts but is persuaded pretty quickly by his wife (Act 1 Scene 7).

Act 2: Scenes 1 to 4

Is this a dagger which I see before me,
The handle toward my hand?

Scene 1   Macbeth visits Banquo, then sees a ghostly dagger

After midnight in Macbeth's castle. Banquo admits to his son Fleance that he cannot sleep and feels uneasy ('*A heavy summons lies like lead upon me*'). Macbeth appears, and Banquo says he has dreamed of the Witches. Macbeth offers his friend power and reward if he sides with him in the future.

Macbeth, now alone, sees a dagger before him, which seems to guide him to Duncan's bedchamber. Then he hears the signal of his wife's bell, and goes to kill King Duncan.

Commentary

- **Banquo's fate** is probably sealed when he refuses to commit himself to Macbeth, saying he will keep his '*allegiance clear*'.

- After initially greeting Banquo as 'a friend', **Macbeth realises he cannot rely on him** for support.

- The appearance of the dagger with blood on it, floating in the air, seems as if it is there to guide Macbeth towards Duncan's bedchamber, and the murder.

Themes

Ambition: Macbeth appeals to Banquo's ambitions and desire for power saying he will receive '*honour*'.

The supernatural: The dagger's ghostly appearance, a '*fatal vision*', is followed by Macbeth talking of '*wicked dreams*', nature seeming '*dead*' whilst '*witchcraft celebrates*'.

Scene 2   Macbeth returns after the murder; Lady Macbeth awaits

Lady Macbeth awaits Macbeth's return. He appears, in a dreadful state, carrying the daggers, unable to think about what he has done. Lady Macbeth takes the daggers and goes to Duncan's room to smear the guards with the blood. She returns, her hands now bloody, too.

Commentary

- Whilst she awaits her husband's news, **Lady Macbeth fears** Macbeth has backed out.

- Macbeth, when he does appear, is **panicky** and **disgusted** by what he has done: '*I am afraid to think what I have done…*'.

- The **tension** is illustrated through the fast pace of the language: '*When?*' '*Now.*' '*As I descended?*' '*Ay.*'.

- Lady Macbeth is **forced to take control** and face the scene of the crime.

- At this stage, Macbeth seems **more traumatised than his wife** who states plainly: '*A foolish thought, to say a sorry sight.*' and '*Consider it not so deeply*'.

Themes

Order and chaos: Macbeth speaks about how he has murdered sleep – how '*Macbeth shall sleep no more.*'

Evil: Macbeth compares himself to a hangman, and mentions how the grooms were praying just before the murder, emphasising how Macbeth is sinning against God. He was unable to say 'Amen'.

O horror, horror, horror,

Scene 3 Macduff discovers the murder

Early the next day, the porter opens the gate to Macduff and Lennox, and jokes with them. Macbeth appears, and Macduff goes to wake the King. Macduff returns in apparent shock, to tell everyone about the murder.

Lady Macbeth appears, and then the King's two sons, Malcolm and Donaldbain enter and are also told the news. Macbeth reappears and admits he has killed the servants in his anger. Malcolm and Donaldbain flee, fearing that they too may die.

Themes

Appearance and reality: The Macbeths both have a lot to hide – and to pretend about. Donaldbain says that '*there's daggers in men's smiles...*' and there is **dramatic irony** as Macduff addresses Lady Macbeth as '*gentle lady*'.

Order and chaos: Lennox reports how '*unruly*' the night has been, full of '*confused events*'.

Commentary

- The porter opens the scene, providing a lighthearted **release of tension**, following the previous scene's events.
- Macduff and Macbeth's strained relationship starts to take shape as **Macduff seems suspicious** about why Macbeth killed the servants.
- Macbeth kills the two servants easily, as he is **gaining courage, but still needs Lady Macbeth's help** to take the attention away from him when he is quizzed on his actions (she faints).

Scene 4 Ross and an Old Man discuss the murder

Outside Macbeth's castle, Ross, and an Old Man speak together. They mention 'unnatural' happenings: the wild behaviour of Duncan's horses, and how the day seems like night it is so dark.

Macduff appears and tells them that the King's sons have fled. They are now suspected of the murder, so Macbeth has been named as the new King. He has gone to Scone to be crowned. Macduff is not going, but is returning home.

Commentary

- This scene deals with **the aftermath**: the 'guilt' of the guards and the escape of the King's sons are reinforced.
- **Nature reflects what is happening** in the action. We hear that darkness '*strangles*' the daylight, for example, and that the heavens are '*troubled with man's act*'. Horses, man's best friend, broke free and '*turned wild in nature*'.
- It is also hinted that **Macduff is not prepared to support Macbeth** as King.

Themes

Order and chaos: Day is like night-time, according to the Old Man, who also describes how gentle or weaker creatures have turned on their masters (a '*...mousing owl...*' kills a hawk, for example). This reflects the unnatural event that has happened – a lesser, seemingly good person killing the King.

The supernatural: (linking with the theme above) Are there forces at work here? What has turned the order upside down so?

Appearance and reality: Nothing is as it seems – or as it could be expected to be.

QUICK CHECK

1. Who is having difficulty sleeping in Act 2 Scene 1?

2. In Act 2 Scene 1, what vision does Macbeth see as he is on the way to Duncan's bed-chamber?

3. In Act 2 Scene 2, who takes the daggers back into Duncan's bed-chamber?

4. How does Macbeth feel immediately after he has killed Duncan?

5. In Act 2 Scene 3, who finds Duncan's body?

6. What other murders happen in this scene, and who commits them?

7. Who seems suspicious about the behaviour of Macbeth?

8. How is the theme of 'appearance and reality' particularly relevant to Act 2 Scene 3?

9. In Act 2 Scene 4, what is strange about the day?

10. Macbeth is going to Scone to be crowned king. Where does Macduff say he is going? Why might this be significant?

Show insight to impress

do brilliantly!

Examiners love 'insight'! This means being able to look beyond the obvious, to why something happens. But how do you show this in the Test? You can **argue against the obvious**. For example, it is usually suggested that Lady Macbeth pretends to faint in Act 2 Scene 3 to draw attention away from her husband after the murder has been discovered. However, you could *suggest* (you don't have to say for certain) that her fainting might be for real, and back it up with reasons:

- Perhaps she suddenly realises the terrible thing she has done?

- Maybe she is shocked by Macbeth's killing of the guards?

- Is she already feeling the first sensations of guilt?

- Or, is the fainting brought on by a sort of nervous excitement?

Help me hence, ho.

Look to the lady.

Here lay Duncan,
His silver skin laced with his golden blood
And his gashed stabs looked like a breach in nature...

THE PLOT: SCENE BY SCENE

on i Secti
Sec2n 1
tion i Sec

Act 3: Scenes 1 to 6

for 't must be done tonight...

Scene 1   Macbeth orders Banquo's murder

Banquo reveals his suspicions about Macbeth in a soliloquy: '*I fear thou played'st most foully...*' for the throne, he says. Macbeth, Lady Macbeth and the other lords appear, and ask Banquo to be present at the banquet that evening. Macbeth speaks of the lies his '*bloody cousins*' (Duncan's sons) are telling in England and in Ireland.

Left alone, Macbeth tells the audience why he must kill Banquo, angry that it is Banquo's children who will eventually be kings of Scotland (according to the Witches). He then speaks to two men (murderers) and persuades them to kill Banquo – and his son Fleance.

Themes

Ambition: Banquo is still thinking about what the Witches promised him. He says they '*set...[him]... up in hope...*'. Macbeth worries about how he is like Mark Antony, and Banquo like Caesar who held Antony back. He seems jealous of Banquo's '*dauntless temper*' and '*wisdom...*'.

Commentary

- This scene shows Macbeth and Banquo **completely divided**.
- Banquo still hopes for the Witches' prophecies to help him.
- Macbeth **now blames Banquo** – saying he committed murder just so Banquo's children can be kings.
- There is **dramatic irony** as Macbeth instructs Banquo '*Fail not our feast*' to which Banquo replies '*My lord, I will not*'. Indeed, he does not (as we see in Act 3 Scene 4).
- In this scene we see that **Macbeth is now acting alone** without consulting his wife: he orders Banquo's murder.

Scene 2   Macbeth and Lady Macbeth discuss their situation

Macbeth and Lady Macbeth meet. Macbeth seems to be thinking too much about what has happened, and appears to regret his actions – it hasn't brought the peace he desired. Lady Macbeth says he must hide his feelings, and he agrees. He then reveals his concerns about Banquo and Fleance, but does *not* tell her what is planned, just that they are taken care of.

Commentary

- The scene provides a bridge between the 'old' Macbeth and the new.

Old Macbeth	New Macbeth
Macbeth is still racked with worry and concern and is still having trouble hiding his inner feelings.	Macbeth is now prepared to act (he arranges for Banquo and his son to be killed) without getting Lady Macbeth's agreement.
Macbeth feels the job is not finished. (He says: '*We have scorched the snake, not killed it...*')	The scene ends with Macbeth giving a speech in which he calls on '*seeling night*' to help him. This is very like Lady Macbeth's call to '*thick night*' in Act 1 Scene 5. Macbeth is now actively embracing evil.

Themes

Good and evil: Macbeth calls upon the '*bloody and invisible hand*' of darkness to hide what is about to take place.

Appearance and reality: Lady Macbeth is still concerned by Macbeth not being able to hide his feelings.

Scene 3   The murder of Banquo

A mysterious third murderer appears, who seems to know a good deal about Banquo's movements. In an isolated place near the royal palace, the murderers ambush Banquo and Fleance, his son. Banquo is killed, but Fleance escapes.

Commentary

- Despite the fact that **Banquo is now dead**, the Witches' prophecy that his children will be kings in the future, can still happen – **Fleance manages to escape**.

- The third murderer's presence: who is he? Some say he might be Macbeth.

Themes

Supernatural: The audience will be aware that the 'Banquo's heirs' prophecy by the Witches, is still very much alive.

Scene 4   The banquet and Banquo's ghost

During a banquet at the royal palace, Macbeth hears news from the first murderer of Banquo's death and Fleance's escape. Lady Macbeth reminds him of his duties as host but as he goes to sit in his place he finds Banquo's ghost, covered in blood, sitting there. Macbeth loses his calm, and shouts at the ghost.

Lady Macbeth tells everyone his behaviour is the result of a childhood illness. The ghost disappears. Macbeth eventually regains control only for the ghost to re-appear. He responds by shouting violently at the ghost, which finally disappears. But the evening is ruined and Lady Macbeth is forced to ask everyone to leave.

Which of you have done this?

Commentary

A King's **banquet** with all the lords of Scotland (except Banquo and Macduff) present should be Macbeth's great moment, but it is **turned into a living nightmare** by:

- the news that Banquo's son has escaped,

- the appearance of **Banquo's ghost** which shakes Macbeth so deeply that he can't bear to look at the evidence of what he's done. '*Avaunt and quit my sight! Let the earth hide thee!*' he says to it.

It is left to Lady Macbeth to pick up the pieces.

Themes

The supernatural: Even Macbeth, who has met the Witches and seen the vision of a dagger, finds this latest vision too much to bear. '*Can such things be…?*' he says.

Order and chaos: It is no coincidence that Banquo chooses to disrupt Macbeth's royal banquet – just when Macbeth hoped he had sorted everything out. Banquo also sits in Macbeth's place. After all, it is his children (according to the Witches) who will one day be kings of Scotland.

Scene 5   Hecate and the three Witches meet

Hecate (the Queen of the Witches) meets the three Witches on a heath. She tells them off for meeting with Macbeth without her being there. Then she sends them away, having arranged that she, and they, will meet Macbeth the following morning.

Commentary

- Hecate tells the Witches (and the audience, of course) that Macbeth will find out more about his future at the next meeting – so, again, we have **dramatic irony** (we know the Witches are plotting, Macbeth does not).

- She also reminds us that Macbeth, like other '*mortals*' (ordinary humans) will '*...spurn fate, scorn death, and bear / His hopes 'bove wisdom, grace, and fear...*' .

Themes

The supernatural: Shakespeare's audiences were fascinated by the spirit world, and would have enjoyed the appearance of the Witches as well as the idea of Hecate directing what might happen to Macbeth.

Scene 6   Lennox reflects and summarises

At the palace, Lennox speaks with 'another lord' about the murderous events. He stops short of accusing Macbeth but does let us know that Macduff '*lives in disgrace*' because he didn't go to Macbeth's great banquet. The other lord tells Lennox that Duncan's son, Malcolm, is staying in England with the English King – Edward. Macduff has gone to seek help from both.

Commentary

- The action so far is **summed up** in this scene – this provides clarity for the audience.

- The scene shows that everyone has to be careful what they say and to whom. Lennox says even Fleance – who fled from the killers of his father – might be accused of being Banquo's murderer! The lord, however, is less cautious, calling Macbeth a '*tyrant*'.

- It also shows that **opposition to Macbeth is growing** – even if it is only outside Scotland, and that Malcolm, Duncan's son, has some powerful allies: the English King, the Earl of Northumberland (Malcolm's uncle) and possibly Macduff.

Themes

Appearance and reality: Lennox is fully aware of the apparent 'facts' about what happened. He explains Macbeth's 'honour killing' of Duncan's servants as '*twould have angered any heart alive / To hear the men deny't*'. We could argue that this suggests he is suspicious of the real reason.

Order and chaos: The lord speaks about how awful things are under Macbeth's control – '*bloody knives*' at banquets, the lack of sleep (due to fear, presumably), the lack of '*free honours*' (in other words, lots of corruption and bribery). This is not the way a proper, ordered state should be governed.

QUICK CHECK

1. What does Macbeth say are his reasons for having Banquo killed in Act 3 Scene 1?

2. In Act 3 Scene 2, Macbeth says that they have '*scorched the snake, not killed it…*'. What does this mean?

3. What is Lady Macbeth still worried about in this scene?

4. In Act 3 Scene 3, Banquo is murdered. Who survives?

5. Why might this be significant?

6. In Act 3 Scene 4, where does Banquo's ghost sit?

7. How does Lady Macbeth try to explain away her husband's wild behaviour?

8. In Act 3 Scene 5, who tells the three Witches off for meeting Macbeth without her being there?

9. In Act 3 Scene 6, the lord who is speaking with Lennox reveals that Malcolm has left Scotland. Where is Malcolm staying?

10. Who has also gone to England to look for support for a war against Macbeth?

Small details = high marks!

do brilliantly!

A good response is one that looks at detail and makes an **interpretation** of it. This is important when there is not much to go on. For example, what do we know about Lennox?

- Lennox appears at Macbeth's castle with Macduff in Act 2 Scene 3. From this we might **infer** that Lennox and Macduff are friends.

- He is present at all the feasts and occasions at the Macbeths' palaces.

- He is reluctant to share his feelings about Macbeth openly.

- **But**…by Act 5 Scene 2, he is siding with the English rebels.

From this, a student might deduce that Lennox is very political and will change sides according to who he thinks is most powerful.

> How it did grieve Macbeth! Did he not straight
> In pious rage, the two delinquents tear,
> That were the slaves of drink and thralls of sleep?
> Was not that nobly done?

What could Lennox be thinking here (Act 3, Scene 6)? Is he behind Macbeth or is he suspicious? Look at the question marks? What could the rhetorical questions indicate?

Act 4: Scenes 1 to 3

> Macbeth shall never vanquished be until Great Birnam Wood to high Dunsinane hill Shall come against him.

Scene 1 Macbeth, the Witches and more prophecies

The Witches wait for Macbeth, chanting spells and creating a disgusting brew. Hecate appears and praises their efforts. Macbeth then arrives and a series of three apparitions (ghosts/visions) appear:

- a head wearing armour, tells Macbeth to '*beware Macduff*'
- '*a bloody child*' tells Macbeth that '*none of woman born*' can harm him
- '*a child crowned, with a tree in his hand*' tells Macbeth that he has nothing to fear until Birnam Wood moves to Dunsinane (Macbeth's castle).

Macbeth is then shown a vision of eight kings, with Banquo's ghost following. Hecate and the Witches vanish after dances and music.

Lennox appears and tells Macbeth that Macduff has fled to England. Macbeth decides there and then to murder Macduff's family.

Themes

The supernatural: The Witches and apparitions dominate what happens, although it is almost as if Macbeth himself has conjured them. He says, '*I conjure you…*'.

Appearance and reality: is symbolised by the three prophecies – each one of them is not what it seems as we will find out in Act 5. What Macbeth is shown, and what is to come, are not the same thing.

Evil: Macbeth's nature is confirmed by his brutal decision to murder the innocent family of Macduff. The Witches summon the forces of evil which are reflected in Macbeth's next actions.

Commentary

- This vitally important scene begins with a powerful chant and spell that create **a dark and forbidding mood**.

- The scene is **visually stunning** with Witches' dances, apparitions, music and chanting. There is **rhythm and tension** in the spells and chants, and the Witches' language is full of **ghastly images**.

- We, with Macbeth, hear of three new prophecies which contain the **seeds of Macbeth's downfall**. Macbeth is established as alone – the sole communicator with the Witches – no one else sees them.

- There is **dramatic irony** also, as Macbeth says '*And damned all those that trust them.*'. This is almost a prophecy in itself. Macbeth continues to trust in the Witches, and this will be his downfall.

- We hear of Macduff's actions and what Macbeth intends to do, which creates **suspense** as we wait for Macbeth's terrible plan to be put into action.

Scene 2   The murders of Macduff's wife and son

At Macduff's castle, Ross tells Macduff's wife that her husband has left for England. She cannot come to terms with this, despite Ross' kind words telling her that Macduff is a decent and wise man. Ross leaves. Lady Macduff and her son talk for a while before a messenger arrives to warn Lady Macduff that she is in danger. But it is too late. The messenger leaves and the murderers enter. They kill her son, then pursue her as she runs off.

Commentary

- **We see how low Macbeth has sunk** – killing an innocent woman and her child.

- This scene provides **a contrast** between the loving, and innocent **Lady Macduff** and the childless **Lady Macbeth** of earlier scenes (see Act 1 Scene 7).

- **Questions are raised** again about the other lords, such as Ross: does he know what is about to happen to Lady Macduff? Who is siding with Macbeth? Is he working completely alone?

Themes

Evil: The contrast between innocence and evil is very clear here.

Appearance and reality: Lady Macduff cannot imagine why she might be in danger as she has '*done no harm*' but then she realises that the world is mad enough that '*to do harm is often laudable...*'. This echoes the Witches' line, '*Fair is foul, and foul is fair...*' from Act 1 Scene 1.

Murder!

Scene 3 Macduff meets Malcolm in England

Macduff visits Malcolm to persuade him to return to Scotland and remove Macbeth but Malcolm is suspicious, and needs to test out whether Macduff really is as decent and loyal as he appears. Malcolm pretends not to be worthy of the throne of Scotland. When he sees Macduff's reaction to this, he tells him the truth: that an English army of ten thousand men, led by Siward (the Earl of Northumberland), has already set off for Scotland.

Ross arrives with reports of the state of Scotland and the murder of Macduff's wife and children. Macduff is devastated, but Malcolm persuades him to turn his anger on Macbeth.

Commentary

- This scene (the longest in the play) is vitally important because of what we learn about Malcom and Macduff:

Malcolm
We are given an insight into the type of king Malcolm might be:
- **wise** – he doesn't trust Macduff to start with
- **determined** – he has already organised forces to recapture the throne
- **persuasive** – he turns Macduff's deep sorrow to passionate anger
  '*Be this the whetstone of your sword, let grief / Convert to anger…*'.

Macduff
We also learn more of Macduff who is a **man of few words**.
He says little here but shows he **cares deeply for Scotland** '*Bleed, bleed, poor country…*'.
He **speaks tenderly and emotionally** about the murder of his children and wife '*All my pretty ones? Did you say all?*'

Themes

Evil: Macbeth is described as '*treacherous*', '*black Macbeth*' and '*devilish*'. This contrasts with the god-like description of the English King.

Ambition: Malcolm says that even people with a '*good and virtuous nature*' might change character when ruled by a tyrant.

Appearance and reality: Malcolm tests Macduff, deliberately pretending to be a worse person than Macbeth. He tells Macduff that he has even more ambition, lusts, desires and weaknesses and that compared with himself, '*black Macbeth will seem as pure as snow…*'.

QUICK CHECK

1. Three apparitions appear to Macbeth in Act 4 Scene 1. What does the third one look like and what is its message?
2. Why is Macbeth so shaken by the appearance of the eight kings?
3. What news is given to Macbeth by Lennox at the end of Act 4 Scene 1?
4. Who visits Lady Macduff and tries to persuade her that her husband is decent? (Act 4 Scene 2)
5. Who else arrives and speaks to her before the murderers enter?
6. Where does Macduff meet Malcolm? (Act 4 Scene 3)
7. What is Malcolm's reaction to Macduff's request that he helps to remove Macbeth?
8. Why does Malcolm say these things?
9. What terrible news does Ross bring near the end of Act 4 Scene 3?
10. How does Malcolm suggest Macduff should use his grief and sorrow?

Plot and language are not separate

do brilliantly!

A key way of gaining the top levels in the Test is to show **how language** can **reflect plot development**.

For example, if you were asked about how tension is built up in Scene 2 (when Lady Macduff is murdered) you could focus on her words: '*to do harm is often laudable…*'. This reminds us (the audience) of what has already happened. People have committed murder for reward, which is an omen of what is to come: the arrival of hired murderers (not Macbeth himself) who kill Lady Macduff and her children. By mentioning this, you are **linking** what happens in **this scene**, with the play **as a whole**.

Remember, the scenes are full of 'echoes' like this – words, phrases and lines that link with **what has happened**, **what is happening** – and **what is going to happen**.

Act 5: Scenes 1 to 9

Scene 1 Lady Macbeth sleepwalks

At Macbeth's castle a Doctor and a Gentlewoman watch Lady Macbeth as she sleepwalks during the night. She rubs her hands continually, as if washing them, and speaks in a wild and painful manner, with references to the murders committed. The doctor concludes that there is little he can do – and that she needs 'divine' rather than medical help.

Commentary

- This scene shows Lady Macbeth's **very sudden descent into madness**.

- Her last appearance was at the banquet, covering up for Macbeth – she still seemed in control then. Perhaps the slaughter of Macduff's family was a step too far. **She has lost control of her husband and, subsequently, of herself**.

Themes

Order and chaos: Lady Macbeth has clearly lost her senses – her mind is '*infected*'. Her sleep is disordered too.

Appearance and reality: The audience will have seen Lady Macbeth as strong and resolute. Now we know that beneath the surface she wasn't as strong as we thought.

Here's the smell of the blood still…

Scene 2   The Scottish lords bring news

Angus, Menteith, Caithness and Lennox (all now opposing Macbeth) inform us of the coming battle. They are going to join the English forces led by Malcolm, Siward and Macduff near Birnam Wood. We are told that Macbeth is strengthening his castle defences but few are now loyal to him.

Commentary

- The scene makes it clear that Macbeth's '*distempered cause*' (sick government) has few supporters, and that **there are strong forces lined up against him.** Interestingly, Malcolm's younger brother, Donaldbain is *not* with him.

Themes

Order and chaos: Lennox makes it clear that the purpose of the fight will be to '*dew the sovereign flower*' (make sure the rightful, healthy plant – Malcolm – succeeds) and '*drown the weeds*' (remove Macbeth).

Ambition: The lords are now on the side of Malcolm and Macduff. We do not know at what point they switched – was it after the murder of Macduff's family?

Scene 3   Macbeth prepares for battle

Fear grips those left in Macbeth's castle, but Macbeth knows he cannot be harmed by anyone '*born of woman*', or until Birnam Wood moves to Dunsinane. Both of which he considers to be impossible.

News comes of the English forces, and Macbeth speaks of having had enough of life. He calls for his armour, and receives news of Lady Macbeth's condition from the Doctor.

Commentary

- This scene shows Macbeth **moving from rage and defiance** ('*I cannot taint with fear...*') **to depressed reflection** ('*I am sick at heart...*'). It also shows how alone he is, surrounded only by frightened servants.

Themes

Order and chaos: Macbeth appears still in control, and is able to give commands ('*Send out more horses; skirr the country round...*') but the truth is that even the Doctor won't stay around – however much money or reward he is given. Macbeth's empire is falling apart.

Scene 4 Macbeth's enemies at Birnam Wood

Malcolm, Siward, Siward's son, Macduff and several Scottish lords are on the march. Malcolm orders the soldiers to cut down boughs from the trees in order to disguise their numbers as they move. It is reported that few remain to support Macbeth except those forced to stay.

Commentary

- In this scene, we are given a glimpse of one of the Witches' later **prophecies coming true**, when the trees from Birnam Wood are cut down.
- We also now see how **hopeless** Macbeth's situation is.

Themes

Appearance and reality: This time it is actual camouflage that hides the reality. Malcolm uses what can be seen (the mass of branches) to hide the reality – his army.

Scene 5 Macbeth hears of Lady Macbeth's death

Macbeth seems to be without fear as he organises his forces to face Malcolm's army.

His preparations are interrupted by '*the cry of women*' and he is soon told that his wife is dead.

A messenger then appears and reports that Birnam Wood is moving towards Dunsinane. Macbeth cannot believe it at first, but the messenger insists it is true. Macbeth leaves, ready to face death.

Commentary

- Macbeth learns of his **wife's death**, but his response is not shock or anger. Instead he **seems to accept his fate wearily**, and has time to reflect on the 'meaning of life'. It is a '*walking shadow, a poor player / That struts and frets his hour upon the stage...*'.
- Macbeth's hour is almost up now, and when he hears about **Birnam Wood moving**, he knows that the Witches' '*equivocation*' (double talk) has tricked him.

Themes

Appearance and reality: We are reminded that the Birnam Wood prophecy was not all that it seemed. Macbeth also describes how man's life seems important, '*full of sound and fury*', but in reality means '*nothing*'. Indeed he has treated others as if their lives meant nothing, and now his own – which had seemed so important – amounts to nothing as his countrymen all wish him dead.

Scene 6   Malcolm's forces in front of Dunsinane Castle

The English army and Malcolm's forces put down the trees and show their full power. Malcolm gives the battle orders and Macduff promises '*blood and death*'.

Commentary

- **The battle-lines are now drawn.** We are told that Siward and his son will lead the first battle. This might make an audience remember the other **fathers and sons** in the story: Duncan and Malcolm, Banquo and Fleance, Macduff and his son.

Themes

Order and chaos: With the battle about to commence, fathers fighting beside their sons and unity among Scotland's subjects, the audience is given a sense of natural order being restored – or that it may well soon be.

Scene 7   Macbeth fights and kills Siward's son

Siward's army has broken through the castle defences and Macbeth faces Siward's son. But remembering the Witches' prophecy he fears no child, and he kills Young Siward. He leaves, and Macduff, Malcolm and Siward enter. There is little or no opposition now and the battle is almost won.

Commentary

- The lack of opposition to Malcolm and his forces emphasises how **unpopular** Macbeth, '*the tyrant*', has become.

- Macduff worries that he won't have the chance of avenging his wife and children, as someone else might have killed Macbeth.

Themes

Appearance and reality: The prophecy appears to be true – Macbeth really cannot be hurt by anyone born of woman – he is surviving the battle. Yet does anyone really believe he can escape?

Scene 8 Macduff kills Macbeth

Macbeth refuses to '*play the Roman fool*' and commit suicide with his own sword, and says he'll fight on. Macduff appears and challenges him.

Macbeth says he has too much of Macduff's blood already on his soul and says that he cannot be harmed by '*one of woman born*'. Macduff reveals he was not born in the usual way but was '*from his mother's womb untimely ripped*' (born by Caesarian section).

Macbeth realises the prophecies have misled him, but decides to fight on. Macduff kills him, and drags his body off–stage.

Commentary

- This is the **climax of the play** – Macduff, who represents the man Macbeth might have been, faces the murderer of his wife and children.

- Macduff almost cannot bring himself to speak ('*I have no words; my voice is in my sword…*') but is able to deliver the **final blow to Macbeth's fate** – the news that he was cut out of his mother's stomach at birth.

Themes

Several themes come together here:

The supernatural: Macbeth remembers the forces that have let him down – he calls them '*juggling fiends*' who talk in '*double sense*'.

Evil: Macbeth is also mocked by Macduff who calls him a '*monster*', a '*tyrant*' and a '*hell-hound*' – a real symbol of evil.

Order and chaos: By killing Macbeth, Macduff restores a little bit of order in his own life – what we might call 'closure'!

Turn, hell-hound, turn!

Scene 9   Malcolm is to be King – peace is restored

Malcolm speaks of the missing 'friends' from the battle and wonders if they are safe. Ross informs Siward that his son is dead but reveals that he died fighting bravely – his wounds were on his front. Then Macduff enters with Macbeth's severed head. Malcolm informs those present that it is believed that Lady Macbeth committed suicide, then he invites everyone present to see him crowned at Scone.

Themes

Order and chaos: the rightful king has been put on the throne so it could be said that order has been restored, and chaos banished. But what about the lords – Ross, Lennox etc? Will they accept the new King? And there is also Donaldbain (Duncan's other son) who did not appear at the battle.

Evil: Malcolm's last speech condemns Macbeth as a '*butcher*' and Lady Macbeth as being like a '*fiend*'. Quite understandably, he has no redeeming words for them at all.

Commentary

This scene demonstrates the rough and bloody nature of civil war.

- First, Siward's son is reported killed. His father seems to accept his son's fate, largely because his son died honourably.
- Then, the head of Macbeth is brought in, providing a suitable conclusion to a play full of blood and killing.

QUICK CHECK

1. Why is Lady Macbeth rubbing her hands when she is sleepwalking? (Act 5 Scene 1)
2. When was the last time we saw Lady Macbeth before this scene?
3. In Act 5 Scene 2 who is definitely *not* with his brother?
4. In Act 5 Scene 3 what is the doctor's decision about whether to stay at Dunsinane or not?
5. Why does Malcolm's army chop down trees from Birnam Wood?
6. Who dies in Act 5 Scene 5?
7. What news does the Messenger bring in Act 5 Scene 5? Why is it significant?
8. Who does Macbeth fight and kill in Act 5 Scene 7?
9. What does Macduff tell Macbeth in Act 5 Scene 8 that means Macbeth is no longer protected by the Witches' words?
10. How did Lady Macbeth die, according to what Malcolm says in the last scene of the play?

Make words live!

do brilliantly!

Students who gain high levels **never forget that this is a play**, and consider the **dramatic effect** of what characters say. So, when Macduff tells Macbeth he was from his mother's womb '*untimely ripped*' and was therefore not born '*of woman*', you can write about why this is a profound moment in the play.

It is Macbeth's last hope – that according to the Witches he cannot be harmed by anyone. Imagine the colour draining from his face as he hears Macduff's words. But, remember the audience. For them, it is equally dramatic because they know that Macbeth is now doomed.

The main characters

Macbeth
**Thane ('lord') of Glamis;
later Thane of Cawdor and King**

Lady Macbeth
Macbeth's wife

'this… butcher and his fiend-like Queen…' (Act 5 Scene 9)

Banquo
A Scottish thane

*'…He hath a wisdom that
doth guide his valour…'*
(Act 3 Scene 1)

Macduff
Thane of Fife

*'I have no words; my
voice is in my sword…'*
(Act 5 Scene 8)

King Duncan
**King of Scotland
at the start of
the play**

'…the gracious Duncan…'
(Act 3 Scene 1)

Malcolm
**Duncan's elder
son and heir**

*'What I am truly is… my
poor country's to command…'*
(Act 4 Scene 3)

The supporting characters

Donaldbain
Duncan's
younger son

The three Witches

Hecate
Queen of the
Witches

Siward
Earl of Northumberland
and his son

Lady Macduff
and her son

Fleance
son of Banquo

The Porter

Scottish Thanes
Ross, Lennox, Menteith, Angus, Caithness

**The three
Murderers**

Seyton
Macbeth's
armour bearer

Doctor

Gentlewoman
to Lady Macbeth

Old Man

Captain
in Duncan's
army

And...
- **An English doctor, from King Edward's court**
- **Various soldiers, lords, attendants and servants**
- **The Witches' apparitions**

Character focus: MACBETH

Who is Macbeth?

- Macbeth is the **Thane (lord) of Glamis** and a **general** in King Duncan's army at the start of the play.
- He is **married to Lady Macbeth**, and lives in Dunsinane Castle.
- He is a **'friend' of Banquo's** – they both appear together at the start of the play.
- Macbeth has **no children**, if Macduff is to be believed: '*He has no children*' he says bitterly in Act 4 Scene 3.
- Macbeth is made **Thane of Cawdor** by King Duncan, and later **becomes King** through murder.

What does Macbeth do in the play?

- Macbeth bravely **fights to defeat** rebels and invaders.
- He **meets the Witches** with Banquo (Act 1 Scene 3) and is told he will be Thane of Cawdor and King.
- He **murders King Duncan**, and his two **servants**. He is **crowned King**.
- He has **Banquo murdered** when he fails to support him.
- He **revisits the Witches** and hears the **new prophecies**. (Act 4 Scene 1)
- As an insurance, he **has Macduff's wife and children killed**. (Act 4 Scene 2)
- He **kills Siward's son** during the siege of Dunsinane Castle, but is finally **killed by Macduff**.

What does Macbeth say and what does this tell us?

Key quotes

> '*Stars, hide your fires,*
> *Let not light see my black and deep desires...*'

(Act 1 Scene 4)

This shows Macbeth's **ambition**. Even at this early stage his thoughts are already turning to murder.

> '*He's here in double trust...*'

(about Duncan, Act 1 Scene 7)

This reveals Macbeth's **uncertainty** at this point about what he should do. It takes Lady Macbeth's taunts to provoke him to action.

> '*Methought I heard a voice cry, 'Sleep no more: / Macbeth does murder sleep...*'

(Macbeth recalling the events before murdering Duncan, Act 2 Scene 2)

These words show the high state of **anxiety**, even **guilt**, that Macbeth is feeling immediately before and after the murder.

> '*Be innocent of the knowledge...*
> *Till thou applaud the deed.*'

(to Lady Macbeth, Act 3 Scene 2)

This shows that Macbeth is **changing**. He is now prepared to act alone, without his wife's knowledge.

> '*I have supped full with horrors;*
> *Direness, familiar to my slaughterous thoughts /*
> *Cannot once start me.*'

(Act 5 Scene 5)

By the end, having committed the worst crimes and sins known to man, Macbeth **no longer feels anything**. He does **not even feel fear**.

What do others say about Macbeth?

Key quotes

'...yet do I fear thy nature,
It is too full o' th' milk of human kindness...'

(Lady Macbeth, Act 1 Scene 5)

Lady Macbeth feels Macbeth **may be too weak** to kill the King, and that she will need to **push him to it.**

'...look like th'innocent flower,
But be the serpent under't.'

(Lady Macbeth to Macbeth, Act 1 Scene 5)

Lady Macbeth feels she needs to **teach Macbeth** how to **disguise his feelings.** Her suspicions of his weakness are proved right by his behaviour both after the murder, and at the banquet.

'...I fear/Thou playd'st most foully for't...'

(Banquo, Act 3 Scene 1)

Banquo **suspects Macbeth** of getting the throne by murder.

'The Thane of Fife had a wife. Where is she / now?'

(Lady Macbeth to Macbeth, in her sleep-walking state, Act 5 Scene 1)

This suggests that even Lady Macbeth is ultimately **appalled** by the lengths her husband went to in order to keep the throne.

'this ...butcher and his fiend-like queen...'

(Malcolm, Act 5 Scene 9)

This is how Malcolm wants us to view Macbeth and his wife: in basic, evil terms. Malcolm sees Macbeth as **evil**, **violent**, and **without pity.**

QUICK CHECK

1. Is Macbeth's first mention in the play in the context of good or evil? Check carefully.

2. When do we *first* see Macbeth and Banquo together?

3. Why is Macbeth initially reluctant to kill Duncan in his speech in Act 1 Scene 7?

4. How does Macbeth feel directly before and after the King's murder?

5. How has he changed by the time his castle is besieged at the end of the play?

6. Who suspects Macbeth '*playd'st most foully...*' for the throne?

7. Why does Macduff have particular cause to hate Macbeth?

8. Whose son does Macbeth kill just before his own death?

Quotations can tell double the information

do brilliantly!

Quotations reveal information to us which is why we use them in essays. For example, we could say Macbeth is an aggressive, thoughtless killer because he is described as a '*dead butcher*' at the end of the play.

But this quotation **tells us just as much** (perhaps more) **about the person who says it** – Malcolm. It is vital, as a new King, that Malcolm ensures that people remember Macbeth badly, so no one feels sympathy for him.

Character focus: Banquo

Who is Banquo?

- Banquo is a **general** in King Duncan's army who fights bravely **alongside Macbeth** against Norwegians and rebel Scots.
- A **'friend' of Macbeth** – they both appear together at the start of the play.
- A **father to one son, Fleance**, and possibly ancestor to future kings (if the prophecy of the Witches is to be believed).
- A **ghost**, after his murder. Or is this a figment of Macbeth's guilty imagination?

What does Banquo do in the play?

- Banquo **fights alongside Macbeth** before the play begins.
- He **meets the Witches** with Macbeth (Act 1 Scene 3) and is told his children, though not he, will be kings.
- He **talks about the future** with Macbeth (Act 2 Scene 1).
- He **dies** after Macbeth orders his murder – Banquo's son escapes (Act 3 Scene 3).
- He **appears as a ghost** at the banquet (Act 3 Scene 4).
- He **appears as an apparition** with the procession of 8 kings (Act 4 Scene 1).

What does Banquo say and what does this tell us?

Key quotes

> 'The instruments of darkness tell us truths; …to betray's…'

(about the Witches, Act 1 Scene 3)

From the start this indicates a **difference** in how **Macbeth and Banquo** view the Witches. Banquo appears **more cautious**. Is this the first thing that comes between them?

> 'A heavy summons lies like lead upon me, And yet I would not sleep…'

(to Fleance, his son, Act 2 Scene 1)

This shows Banquo **feels uneasy** – does he **already suspect** Macbeth of planning murder? Or is he considering what action he might take? After all, the Witches have promised him things, too. Even though they say he will be '*not so happy*' as Macbeth.

> '…but still keep / My bosom franchised and allegiance clear…'

(to Macbeth, Act 2 Scene 1)

Banquo **refuses to give his support** (his '*allegiance*') to Macbeth when he asks for it. Banquo probably signs his own death warrant by not pledging support to Macbeth.

> '…I fear / Thou played'st most foully for't…'

(about Macbeth and the King's murder, Act 3 Scene 1)

This shows **Banquo knows what happened**. It is for this reason that Macbeth cannot let him live.

What do others say about Banquo?

Key quotes

'Lesser than Macbeth, and greater...'

(First Witch to Banquo, Act 1 Scene 3)

This indicates where **the trouble between Macbeth and Banquo** might start. What are they to think of the Witches' promises?

'Noble Banquo...let me enfold thee,
And hold thee to my heart.'

(King Duncan to Banquo, Act 1 Scene 4)

This shows how **well regarded Banquo** is by Duncan, although, unlike Macbeth, he is not rewarded or promoted. The word *'noble'* is often used – and Macbeth uses it almost as a criticism, later.

'If you shall cleave to my consent…
It shall make honour for you.'

(Macbeth to Banquo, Act 2 Scene 1)

This is a **key moment**, when **Macbeth asks Banquo to support him** in the future, it is a turning point for both of them. Banquo appears to **reject him** and this leads to his own death and Macbeth's further descent into evil.

'Hence, horrible shadow,
Unreal mock'ry, hence'

(Macbeth to Banquo's ghost, Act 3 Scene 4)

Banquo has the last laugh from **beyond the grave**. This echoes the fact that long after Macbeth is dead, Banquo's own children will be the fathers of future kings, 'mocking' Macbeth. Banquo is, indeed, as the Witches say, *'Not so happy, yet much happier'* than Macbeth.

Have your own views

do brilliantly!

One key to higher levels is to **think for yourself**, not just follow what you have been told about a character.

For example, is Banquo really so noble? Read what one young actor, who played the part recently, said…

'…The traditional view of Banquo is that he's the opposite of Macbeth – that Macbeth becomes all that is evil and Banquo is all that is good – but I didn't want to play him like that. He's a warrior just like Macbeth, a killer of men…

…In his soliloquy, Banquo (in Act 3 Scene 1) wishes the Weird Sisters' prophesies to work for him as they have for Macbeth ("may they not…set me up in hope?") so it's by no means cut and dried where Banquo's ambition might take him…'
Barnaby Kay

May they not be my oracles as well, And set me up in hope? But hush, no more.

QUICK CHECK

1. Why does Duncan call Banquo 'noble'?
2. When do we first see Macbeth and Banquo together?
3. What is Banquo's reaction to what the witches promise?
4. How does King Duncan react to Banquo when they meet after the battle?
5. Why does Macbeth have Banquo killed?
6. Who escapes?
7. What is Banquo's last appearance in the play?

Try to find a quote to support each of your answers.

Remember! In the Shakespeare Paper you will be expected to support everything you write by reference to quotations or scenes from the play. You do not just 'tell the story'.

Character focus: Lady Macbeth

Who is Lady Macbeth?

- She is **Macbeth's wife**.
- The **wife of a Thane** (a Scottish lord) so therefore respected and highly-ranked in Scottish society.

> Hie thee hither,
> That I may pour my
> spirits in thine ear…

What does Lady Macbeth do in the play?

- Lady Macbeth meets Macbeth on his return from meeting the King (Act 1 Scene 5).
- She welcomes Duncan and his court (Act 1 Scene 6).
- She persuades a shaky Macbeth to go through with the murder (Act 1 Scene 7).
- She returns to Duncan's room, after the murder to smear blood on the servants (Act 2 Scene 2).
- She faints to prevent Macbeth facing awkward questions (Act 2 Scene 3).
- She lies for Macbeth at the banquet when he sees the ghost of Banquo (Act 3 Scene 4).
- She sleepwalks, 'washing' her hands of blood (Act 5 Scene 1).
- She is reported to have committed suicide (Act 5 Scene 9).

What does Lady Macbeth say and what does this tell us?

Key quotes

Lady Macbeth's first appearance is in **Act 1 Scene 5** reading Macbeth's letter to her which tells of the Witches' prophesies, and his ambitions, but she says of her husband:

> '…yet do I fear thy nature,
> It is too full o'th'milk of human kindness…'

She has **already decided** to support Macbeth's ambitions, but she fears he will not have the ruthlessness needed.

Later in the same scene, Lady Macbeth realises she needs strength, so she calls on evil spirits to help her.

> '…Come, you spirits
> That tend on mortal thoughts, unsex me here /
> And fill me from the crown to the toe topfull
> Of direst cruelty…'

This shows **cold-blooded cruelty**. She wants to remove her feminine side.

When Macbeth expresses doubt about going through with the murder in **Act 1 Scene 7**, Lady Macbeth **taunts** him, saying he is not a man:

> 'What beast was't then
> That made you break this enterprise to me?'
> And:
> '…Art thou afeard…?'

While she waits for Macbeth to return from killing Duncan in **Act 2 Scene 2** we see the first glimpse of a **weaker side** to her. She says:

> 'Had he (the King) not resembled / My father as he slept, I had done't.'

because he looked too much like her own father.

By **Act 5 Scene 1**, this element of weakness grows to the point that she is **sleepwalking**, speaking of the (imaginary) blood she cannot remove from her hands.

> 'What, will these hands ne'er be clean?'
> And:
> '…all the perfumes of Arabia will not sweeten this little hand…'

What do others say about Lady Macbeth?

Duncan calls Lady Macbeth, '*our honoured hostess*' and '*Fair and noble hostess*' (**Act 1 Scene 6**) when he arrives at the Macbeths' castle. This shows how good she is at **hiding her true feelings** and plans.

Macbeth cannot believe how **cold-blooded** Lady Macbeth appears to be in **Act 1 Scene 7**. He says to her:

> '*Bring forth men-children only,*
> *For thy undaunted mettle should compose*
> *Nothing but males.*'.

Macbeth means, 'When you have children, they will be boys because there is **no trace of femininity** in you.'

In **Act 3 Scene 2**, Macbeth later reveals that he is worried by what Banquo might do. He tells Lady Macbeth he has something planned for Banquo and his son, Fleance. Crucially, however, he **does not** tell her the details:

> '*Be innocent of the knowledge, dearest chuck,*
> *Till thou applaud the deed.*'

This shows **Macbeth** is now **the driving force** in the relationship. He has decided his wife does not need to know until the murder has been committed.

In **Act 5 Scene 1** we can see that Lady Macbeth is now **a changed person** from what the Doctor says while watching her sleepwalk:

> '*What a sigh is there? The heart is sorely charged.*'

This shows that Lady Macbeth **feels guilt**.

Language reveals change in characters

do brilliantly!

You need to focus on specific lines and phrases and say what they tell us. Equally importantly try to say how **one line tells us something** – and how a **later line shows a change** or development.

For example, at the start of the play Lady Macbeth says to Macbeth that the '*...dead are but as pictures...*' (Act 2 Scene 2). This can be linked to her reference to other dead people later, when she is sleepwalking (Act 5 Scene 1). You could comment on how she talks about the dead in general (as above) but later they have names – it's become personal: '*The Thane of Fife* (Macduff) *had a wife. Where is she now?*'.

QUICK CHECK

1. Who does Lady Macbeth fear has too much of the '*milk of human kindness*'?

2. What does she want removed from her body in Act 1 Scene 5?

3. Why does she say she could not have killed Duncan herself? (Act 2 Scene 2)

4. What does this, perhaps, show about her?

5. What does she imagine is on her hands in the sleepwalking scene? (Act 5 Scene 1)

6. How does King Duncan describe her when he arrives at the castle in Act 1 Scene 6?

7. When do we find out that Lady Macbeth has committed suicide?

8. What might have been the event that finally made Lady Macbeth lose her mind?

Character focus: Macduff

Turn, hell-hound, turn.

What does Macduff do in the play?

- Macduff arrives at Macbeth's castle (Act 2 Scene 3) and is the first person to see the King's body when he goes to wake him.

- He asks Macbeth awkward questions after the murder (Act 2 Scene 3). He wants to know why he killed the grooms ('*Wherefore did you so?*') He is already suspicious.

- He refuses to go to Scone to see Macbeth crowned. (Act 2 Scene 4)

- He goes to England, and refuses to return to Scotland (Act 3 Scene 6) angering Macbeth.

- He hears that his wife and children were murdered on Macbeth's orders (Act 4 Scene 2).

- He meets with Malcolm, in England, and joins the army which attacks Macbeth. (Act 4 Scene 3)

- He returns to kill Macbeth in Act 5 Scene 4. This fulfils the prophecy that no one '*of woman born*' can harm Macbeth. In Act 5 Scene 8 he tells Macbeth he was '*untimely ripped*' from his mother's body – Macduff was born by a Caesarean section and was therefore not born naturally (of woman).

Who is Macduff?

- Macduff is Thane of Fife.
- He is married to Lady Macduff.
- He has children.

Macduff's character

Macduff is a man of few words but strong feelings.

Evidence

When Macbeth gives a 'flowery' speech telling Malcolm and Donaldbain their father is dead, Macduff breaks in and says bluntly:

'*Your royal father's murdered.*'

(Act 2 Scene 3).

When Macduff learns his wife and children have been slaughtered his words are full of disbelief, and are tender, showing that he is heartbroken:

'*What, all my pretty chickens and their dam, / At one fell swoop?*'

(Act 4 Scene 3).

Macduff tells Macbeth when he meets him:

'*I have no words my voice is in my sword;*'

(Act 5 Scene 8).
He is a fighter, ready for revenge.

Character focus: Malcolm

Who is Malcolm?

- Malcolm is the **elder son of King Duncan**.
- He is **made heir** to the throne (and given the title 'The Prince of Cumberland').
- He has a younger brother, Donaldbain.

> Let's make us med'cines of our great revenge...

What does Malcolm do in the play?

- Malcolm first appears in Act 1 Scene 4, when he is made next-in-line for the throne. Macbeth realises that Malcolm stands in his way ('*that is a step / On which I must fall down, or else o'erleap, / For in my way it lies.*').

- He **flees from Macbeth's castle** with Donaldbain in Act 2 Scene 3 after their father's murder, fearing they might be next. Malcolm **goes to England**.

- He **is blamed** (by Macbeth), along with Donaldbain, for their father's murder (Act 3 Scene 1).

- He **meets with Macduff** in Act 4 Scene 3, and they decide to return to Scotland with a joint army.

- He **leads an army against Macbeth**. In Act 5 Scene 4 he orders the **cutting down of trees in Birnam Wood** to disguise his army's numbers.

- He **is restored to the throne** in Act 5 Scene 9 after Macbeth's defeat and death.

Malcolm's character

Malcolm is a **clever** young man who through experience, **learns not to trust**. He is **politically aware**.

Evidence

Malcolm realises quickly that he is not safe at Macbeth's castle and that **people cannot be trusted**. He says to his brother:

> '*To show an unfelt sorrow is an office… Which the false man does easy.*'
>
> (Act 2 Scene 3)

He goes to England to raise support from the English King. This shows **good political judgement**.

He shows he can handle situations carefully when he tests Macduff by pretending to be as bad as Macbeth (Act 4 Scene 3), then uses Macduff's despair at his family's murder to turn it against Macbeth. He says,

> '*…let grief / Convert to anger; blunt not the heart, enrage it.*'.

He shows himself to be a **clever leader** when he orders the trees of Birnam Wood to be cut down to hide the army's numbers in Act 5 Scene 4.

4 · Key themes

AMBITION

Ambition is a character's desire to get or achieve something he or she wants – it is about becoming or having something greater. In Shakespeare's plays, ambition is often connected to **power**, **wealth** or **influence**. We see this in *Macbeth*.

> Who in the play wants or desires these things?

> Macbeth for a start.

> What is his ambition?

> To become King. This will bring him wealth, power and influence – or so he thinks.

> How do we know he is ambitious?

> Evidence!

What happens?	What **Macbeth** says	What this means
Act 1 Scene 3 Macbeth is told he has been made Thane of Cawdor. The Witches have also predicted he will be king.	Macbeth says: *'...why do I yield to that suggestion, / Whose horrid image doth unfix my hair...'* .	Macbeth is already considering the *'horrid'* thought of killing the King – he says he is *'yielding'*, i.e. giving in to that *'suggestion'*.
Act 1 Scene 4 Duncan announces that Malcolm, his son, is to be made 'Prince of Cumberland' and heir to the throne. Macbeth is not happy.	Macbeth says: *'that is a step / On which I must fall down, or else o'erleap, / For in my way it lies...'*.	Macbeth is saying that he needs to seize power in such a way that Malcolm is no longer a rival. This is pretty ambitious – kill the King, *and* get rid of the competition!
Act 1 Scene 7 Macbeth speaks to himself, trying to decide whether he should go through with Duncan's murder.	Macbeth says: *'I have no spur / To prick the sides of my intent, but only / Vaulting ambition...'*.	The only thing that Macbeth has to *'spur'* him on is his high (*'vaulting'*) ambition. He does not want to do the deed, but ambition is propelling him.
Act 3 Scene 1 Macbeth considers how Banquo has more to gain from the murder. After all, it is Banquo's children that the Witches have said will be kings in the future.	Macbeth says about Banquo: *'under him / My genius is rebuked, as it is said / Mark Antony's was by Caesar...'*.	Macbeth is comparing himself to the Roman general Mark Antony who was held back from *his* ambitions by Octavius Caesar.

Is Macbeth the *only* ambitious person in the play?

No, there is Lady Macbeth. Some say she is even *more* ambitious than her husband. There is evidence for this, too.

What happens?	**What Lady Macbeth says**	**What this means**
Act 1 Scene 5		
Lady Macbeth reads Macbeth's letter telling her about the witches' prophesies. She immediately decides that Macbeth will become King.	▶ Lady Macbeth says that Macbeth: *'shalt be / What thou art promised...'*	▶ Lady Macbeth decides straight away that Macbeth will achieve what the Witches have prophesied.
	▶ *'I do fear thy nature, / It is too full of the milk of human kindness...'*	▶ However, Lady Macbeth recognises that Macbeth may not be mentally strong enough – or not evil enough – to go through with the murder.
	▶ *'That I might pour mine spirits in thine ear…'.*	▶ She realises that she will have to encourage him and that *her* ambition will have to support him.
Act 1 Scene 7		
Lady Macbeth tries to urge Macbeth to go through with his 'promise' to kill the King. She is still worried he is not ruthless or ambitious enough.	▶ Lady Macbeth says she would have taken the baby she nursed and would have *'dashed the brains out...'* while she was feeding him!	▶ Lady Macbeth would not let anything – however innocent – stand in the way of her ambition. She says this to stir Macbeth, challenging his manhood, as if to say – if a woman like me could do this…!
Act 2 Scene 2		
Just after Macbeth has murdered Duncan, he returns and starts panicking. Lady Macbeth takes control in order to see that the plan goes well.	▶ Lady Macbeth says she will: *'gild the faces of the grooms withal / For it must seem their guilt...'.*	▶ Here, Lady Macbeth takes control. She has to paint (*'gild'*) the faces of the grooms (servants) with blood as Macbeth cannot bring himself to do it. Without his wife, where would Macbeth be? She drugged the servants and is now finishing his job for him.

QUICK CHECK

1. When does Macbeth first consider killing Duncan?
2. Which of the King's sons is blocking Macbeth's ambition (to become King)?
3. Which famous Roman does Macbeth compare himself to?
4. How does Lady Macbeth find out about the Witches' prophesies?
5. What would Lady Macbeth be prepared to do to fulfil her ambition, or promise?
6. What actions does Lady Macbeth take to make sure the murder is successful?

Widen your ideas

do brilliantly!

It is easy to keep to obvious ideas when writing about a theme, but is there more you can say?

For example, are Macbeth and Lady Macbeth the only ambitious characters in the play? What about the **original Thane of Cawdor**? He wasn't loyal to Duncan. Perhaps he, too, wanted to be king?

And Banquo? At the start of Act 3 Scene 1 he knows what Macbeth has done, but seems more concerned with what the Witches promised him. *'...it was said... myself should be the root and father / Of many kings.'* Clearly, he is thinking about **his own** ambitions.

41

ORDER AND CHAOS

Order and chaos means the way things naturally are (**order**) and how things are when order is turned upside down (**chaos**). In Shakespeare's times, the King was very much a part of the **natural order**, as he was believed to have been **chosen by God**. The King had a **divine right to rule**.

> So, *Macbeth* is about the **chaos** that is created when that **order** is challenged, right?

> Yes. *Macbeth* is about a **decent King**, Duncan, who is **wrongly removed** from the throne. It's about the **chaos** which follows this crime and the reinstatement of **order** and the **rightful King**.

> Who is **responsible** for the **chaos**, then?

> It's **Macbeth** who creates most of the **chaos** and **disorder** in the play through his action of killing the King but remember that he only acts after hearing the Witche's prophesies. **Other characters** create chaos and disorder too.

What happens?	What is said?	What this means
Act 1 Scene 1		
The Witches create chaos The Witches speak about how normal things (order) will be turned upside down. There is even chaotic weather around them.	The Witches chant: *'Fair is foul, and foul is fair...'*	This means that what is evil is good, and what is good is evil. This sets the tone of the play and indicates that chaos is in the air. This is also an example of the theme of **appearance and reality** (see pages 44–45).
Act 1 Scene 1		
The play starts with civil war The Witches mention 'the battle' – meaning the civil war sweeping through Scotland. War = **chaos**.	The Witches chant: *'When the battle's lost, and won.'*	The Witches are referring to the battle between the Norwegians, the rebels, and Duncan's army led by Macbeth. The play begins, therefore, with **chaos**.
Act 1 Scene 7		
The killing of Duncan is unnatural and against the rightful order Macbeth recognises that if he kills Duncan, he will create a dreadful reaction as he will have killed the rightful King.	Macbeth (soliloquy): *'First, as I am his kinsman and his subject, / Strong both against the deed...'*	Macbeth recognises that it goes against the natural order to kill the King.
	'...as his host, / Who should against his murderer shut the door...'	There is another reason for the murder to be unnatural – Macbeth is Duncan's host.
	'...his virtues / Will plead like angels, trumpet-tongued, against / The deep-damnation of his taking off.'	Thirdly, Macbeth knows that Duncan is a good man. He knows that *'deep damnation'* will follow the *'horrid deed'*.

What happens?	**What is said?**	**What this means**

Act 2 Scene 2

Macbeth destroys natural sleep

After killing Duncan, Macbeth is troubled by the idea that he has killed sleep.

▶ Macbeth says:
'*Methought I heard a voice cry, 'Sleep no more: / Macbeth does murder sleep', the innocent sleep.*'

▶ We know that Macbeth has killed Duncan while he slept. Macbeth cannot stop thinking about what he has done – and its effects. Sleep gives life; take away sleep and you have insanity and chaos.

Act 2 Scene 4

The natural order is thrown into confusion by the murder

On the morning following the murder, the Old Man and Ross describe how nature was thrown into confusion (**disorder/chaos**). This mirrors what has happened – the murder of a decent king.

▶ Ross says:
'*dark night strangles the travelling lamp*' (the sun).

▶ The Old Man says:
'*A falcon tow'ring in her pride of place / Was by a mousing owl hawked at and killed.*'

▶ Ross describes how it is supposed to be daytime, but is more like night as it is so dark.

▶ The Old Man describes how an owl killed a more powerful bird – a falcon. Does this make you think of anyone?

In both these examples we see how the **natural order** of things has been *reversed*.

Act 3 Scene 4

Macbeth loses control

Macbeth loses control at the banquet when he sees Banquo's ghost.

▶ Lady Macbeth says to her husband:
'*You have displaced the mirth, broke the good meeting, / With most admired disorder.*'

▶ Here, Lady Macbeth speaks firmly to Macbeth, after he has created a scene at the banquet. She tells him that the meal is ruined: **chaos replaces order**.

Act 5 Scene 1

Lady Macbeth goes mad

The final act of personal disorder – Lady Macbeth loses her mind as her guilt for what has happened sends her mad.

▶ The doctor says that:
'*unnatural deeds / Do breed unnatural troubles*'.

▶ In other words, the doctor is saying that her pain – the **chaos in her mind** – is a result of the terrible crimes she has committed.

QUICK CHECK

1. How is Macbeth upsetting the 'natural order' by killing Duncan?

2. What do the Witches say that hints at how good things will be turned upside down?

3. What does Macbeth keep on talking about after he has killed Duncan? (Act 2 Scene 2)

4. Why does Macbeth lose control in Act 3 Scene 4?

Draw contrasts

do brilliantly!

Most students find it easy to show the contrasts between order and chaos in the play. But you could go further.

Consider what might happen after the play. Although order is restored at the end, do you think Malcolm will suffer the same fate as his father?

Think about:
- whether Malcolm has **learned anything** from his experiences?
- whether he is **as trusting** as his father was.

APPEARANCE AND REALITY

Appearance and reality refers to the way in which things or people **seem to mean one thing, but actually mean another**. It is about disguise, hiding the truth and giving misleading information.

Is this theme important in *Macbeth*?

Yes, very important. The idea of things not being as they seem is indicated by the **Witches' words** in Act 1 Scene 1: *'Fair is foul, and foul is fair…'*

What does this mean?

This means that things that **appear** good are really bad and things that **appear** bad are really good.

What happens?	What is said about the first Thane of Cawdor?	Appearance/Reality?
Act 1 Scene 2 Ross comes back from battle with reports of Cawdor's treachery.	Ross says: *'Assisted by that most disloyal traitor, / The Thane of Cawdor…'*	Cawdor is a 'traitor'. Therefore, he was **once trusted** (*'an absolute trust'*, Act 1 Scene 4), but has **turned against** the King.
Act 1 Scene 2 Duncan orders Cawdor's death and declares Macbeth the new Thane of Cawdor.	Duncan says: *'No more that Thane of Cawdor shall deceive / Our bosom interest.'* He continues: *'Go pronounce his present death, / And with his former title greet Macbeth.'*	Duncan wants men he can trust; he no longer wants to be 'deceived' by the Thane of Cawdor. But who does he choose as the new thane? …Macbeth! It **appears** that the thane will no longer deceive… but the reality?

What happens?	What is said about Macbeth?	Appearance/Reality
Act 1 Scene 4 Duncan hears of Macbeth's heroism on the battlefield.	Duncan calls Macbeth: *'worthiest cousin'.*	**Appearance:** Duncan sees Macbeth as a hero and saviour of Scotland. **Reality:** The thought of killing Duncan has already crossed Macbeth's mind. He has referred to the *'horrid image'* in Act 1 Scene 3, meaning the picture in his mind of killing Duncan.

What happens?	What is said about Macbeth's castle?	Appearance/Reality
Act 1 Scene 6 King Duncan arrives at Macbeth's castle.	Duncan says: *'This castle hath a pleasant seat; the air / Nimbly and sweetly recommends itself / Unto our gentle senses'.*	**Appearance:** The castle has something gentle about it and Duncan finds it very pleasant. **Reality:** Duncan has invited himself to the place where he will meet his death.

The language of disguise (hiding the reality)

The play is full of references to how characters **must hide their true feelings**, or that people's appearances **cannot be trusted**.

What is said?	What this means
Act 1 Scene 6	
Lady Macbeth tells Macbeth that he must hide his murderous ambitions: *'look like th'innocent flower, / But be the serpent under't.'*	Lady Macbeth says that Macbeth should pretend to be gentle but really be poisonous – hide the fact that he is going to kill Duncan.
Act 1 Scene 7	
After talking to his wife, Macbeth decides to go through with the murder, and to carry on as normal: *'False face must hide what the false heart doth know'.*	Macbeth means that his lying heart must be disguised by his lying face – he must hide what he is planning to do.
Act 2 Scene 3	
Donaldbain (Duncan's younger son) shares his fears with Malcolm: *'There's daggers in men's smiles.'*	Donaldbain means here that people's smiles are not to be trusted. He is saying that, although faces are smiling, there is murder on their minds.

The Witches' prophecies

On the surface, many of the Witches' prophecies appear to offer good things but, in reality, they hide a darker, more evil truth. Look at these two examples.

What the Witches say	What this means	Appearance/Reality
Act 4 Scene 1		
'…none of woman born / Shall harm Macbeth.'	No one who has been born from a woman can kill Macbeth.	**Appearance:** No one can kill Macbeth. **Reality:** Macduff was born by Caesarean section – so he can!
Act 4 Scene 1		
'Macbeth shall never vanquished be until / Great Birnam Wood to high Dunsinane hill / Shall come against him.'	Macbeth will only be beaten when Birnam wood moves to Dunsinane hill (where his castle is).	**Appearance:** Macbeth cannot be beaten as a wood cannot move. **Reality:** Malcolm and Macduff and their army cut down the branches of the trees and use them as a disguise.

QUICK CHECK

1. In what way is the first Thane of Cawdor a traitor?
2. What words does Duncan use to praise Macbeth?
3. How is Duncan's view of Macbeth's castle misguided?
4. Who says Macbeth must '*look like th'innocent flower…*'?
5. Why is Macduff an example of the theme of appearance and reality?

Tension for effect

do brilliantly!

If you can comment on how a particular moment in the play **creates a dramatic effect**, then you show you really **understand the craft of the writer**.

For example, think what effect is created by Macbeth losing his cool when he sees the ghost. Do the audience want him to be caught? That wouldn't be much fun!

GOOD AND EVIL

Good and **evil** are quite easy concepts to explain. The good and the bad, the divine and the satanic, light and dark are what we mean by the **opposing forces** of **good and evil**.

The language of good and evil

If you look through the play, you will find that it is filled with the **language of good and evil**. There are countless references to angels, heaven, evil and the dark, for example:

- Macbeth compares Duncan's virtues to '*angels, trumpet-tongued*' (Act 1 Scene 7)
- Macduff describes how '*sacrilegious* murder hath broke ope the **Lord's anointed temple**' when he discovers Duncan's body (Act 2 Scene 3)
- Macbeth is called '*devilish*' (Act 4 Scene 3), a '*hell-hound*' (Act 5 Scene 8) and a '*butcher*' (Act 5 Scene 9).

> *Macbeth* is all about evil, that's obvious! Macbeth is an evil character – he commits murder to get what he wants.

> Yes, but there is **a lot of good** in the play as well. Think about it!

> OK, the good characters … Macduff, Malcolm …

> Yes, **Macduff** and **Malcolm** are 'good' characters, but there are others.

Characters who represent 'goodness'

In most cases, the people Macbeth kills are characters who are seen as **good** and **innocent**. We know that from the language Shakespeare uses to describe them – evidence!

Who is murdered?	How are they described?	What this means
King Duncan	Macbeth calls him '*gracious*' (Act 3 Scene 1), and says his virtues '*will plead like angels*' (Act 1 Scene 7).	'Grace' and 'virtue', and being like an '**angel**' all make Duncan sound **saintly**.
Banquo	Duncan calls him '*noble*' and '*worthy*'. (Act 1 Scene 4)	The saintly Duncan praises Banquo. **Even Macbeth** says he is '*dauntless*' and has '*valour*' (bravery). (Act 3 Scene 1)
Lady Macduff and her children	When Macduff hears his family have been slaughtered he says: '*What, all my pretty chickens and their dam / At one fell swoop?*' (Act 4 Scene 3).	Macduff compares his wife and children to a mother hen and her little chicks. As Shakespeare describes them as so **innocent**, murdering them could not seem more evil.

Malcolm and Macduff

Malcolm and Macduff are both characters who represent **good** in *Macbeth*. They, unlike Duncan, Banquo and Macduff's family, outlive the tyrant Macbeth.

Malcolm

Malcolm is **good** because:
- he says that he takes as much pleasure in *'truth'* as in *'life'*, (Act 4 Scene 3)
- he regains his rightful throne
- he overthrows Macbeth
- he restores order to Scotland.

Remember Malcolm is less 'innocent' than his father. He has had to learn not to trust – which is why he tests Macduff's loyalty in Act 4 Scene 3.

...this noble passion... hath ...reconciled my thoughts to thy good truth and honour.

Macduff

Macduff is **good** because:
- he suspects Macbeth from the start (he refuses to go to Scone to see Macbeth crowned in Act 2 Scene 4)
- he bravely fights Macbeth and kills him.

On the other hand, some might say he should be blamed for leaving his wife and children unprotected.

What, all my pretty chickens...?

Is Lady Macbeth evil?

Come, you spirits... And fill me from the crown to the toe topful Of direst cruelty...

Lady Macbeth is **evil** because:
- she plans the murder of Duncan
- she calls on evil spirits to help her
- she urges Macbeth on when he has doubts
- she lies to cover up when Macbeth loses control.

However she does appear to feel **guilt**. She sleepwalks and seems to be having nightmares about what she has done (Act 5 Scene 1). Later, she commits suicide. Are these the actions of a truly evil person?

QUICK CHECK

1. What evidence is there that even Macbeth thinks of Duncan as innocent and good?
2. Who is described as being like innocent little chicks?
3. How is Malcolm *less* innocent than his father?
4. Who refuses to go to Scone to see Macbeth crowned?
5. Who calls on evil spirits to fill her body with *'direst cruelty'*?

Don't be scared to question

do brilliantly!

Students aiming for higher levels should raise questions.

For example, we don't know if **the Thanes** (Ross, Lennox etc) *actually* support Malcolm or just swap sides to follow whoever is most likely to win.

The Witches must be evil, surely? But they don't kill Duncan, or Banquo or Macduff's children. And they don't actually lie to Macbeth. He is the one who chooses to commit murder.

THE SUPERNATURAL

Supernatural means anything that is not from this world. The prefix 'super' means above 'natura', nature. So, anything to do with witches, demons and spells is said to be **supernatural**.

> The play *Macbeth* is full of things which could be described as 'supernatural.'

> That's right, the play even begins with the supernatural, with the Witches. They set the tone, right at the beginning.

References to the supernatural

Macbeth contains many references to the supernatural, such as:
- prophecies/looking into the future
- strange visions
- ghosts
- demonic possession.

The Three Witches

The Witches even look supernatural. Banquo describes them as looking: '*So withered and so wild...*' Macbeth calls them: '*secret, black, and midnight hags...*'

What happens?	What the Witches say	What this means
The Witches appear in Act 1 Scene 1 calling on their 'familiars'. They seem to know that they will meet Macbeth later.	The Third Witch says: '*There to meet with Macbeth*'.	The Witches demonstrate their supernatural powers in the first scene of the play.
They then appear in Act 1 Scene 3, and give riddle-like information to Macbeth and Banquo.	To Banquo the First Witch says: '*Lesser than Macbeth, and greater*'.	This is misleading and neither Banquo nor Macbeth can be sure what it means, although we find out later in the play.
Later, the Witches meet Hecate – Queen of the Witches, and then shortly afterwards (Act 4 Scene 1) they provide more information to Macbeth and a show of apparitions.	One of the Witches apparitions tells Macbeth: '*Macbeth shall never vanquished be until / Great Birnam Wood to high Dunsinane hill / Shall come against him.*'	Again, the Witches provide misleading information. It seems that this would mean Macbeth was safe, but that is not the case.

Other strange visions and ghosts

● **Macbeth's ghostly dagger** – Act 2 Scene 1

A dagger appears before Macbeth's eyes and appears to show him the way to Duncan's bed-chamber. But even Macbeth is not sure if this is supernatural – or something his own mind has created.

> '...art thou but / A dagger of the mind...'

● **Banquo's ghost** – Act 3 Scene 4

As Macbeth goes to sit in his place at the banquet, the ghost of Banquo appears. Macbeth is sure that the ghost is *not* a figment of his own imagination. He tells Lady Macbeth:

> 'Stones have been known to move and trees to speak.'

● **The apparitions** – Act 4 Scene 1

The Witches show Macbeth three apparitions, (the last two being children) each of whom tells Macbeth something (to beware Macduff; to fear no one born of woman; and that he is safe until Birnam Wood moves). There is then the show of eight kings, and the reappearance of Banquo's ghost. All these apparitions act as a warning to Macbeth, only there is a surprise in each.

QUICK CHECK

1. Who sees the three Witches?
2. We are told they are Witches, but what else in their behaviour and what they say makes it obvious?
3. Where does the dagger Macbeth sees seem to be leading him?
4. What/who appears in Act 3 Scene 4?
5. What do we later learn about two of the apparitions shown to Macbeth in Act 4 Scene 1?

Is Macbeth possessed by the devil?

do brilliantly !

You may wish to make a point about your selected scene. But can you **trace its roots** elsewhere? If you can, then this is very impressive.

Imagine you wanted to 'prove' Macbeth was possessed by the devil, you could mention:

Act 1 Scene 3
Macbeth is '*rapt*' (lost in a sort of trance) after seeing the Witches.

Act 2 Scene 2
Macbeth can't say the word 'Amen', or pray, it is as if he is stopped by some demonic force.

Act 4 Scene 1
Macbeth says to the Witches:
'*I conjure you....answer me...*' It is as if *he* is like the devil.

Use of language

> **What does 'language' mean?**

> The 'language' of any text means the way a writer **uses** words and phrases to get across his/her message. Looking at language means not just looking at **what** is said, but **how** it is said and the **effect that this has on the audience**.

> **OK, but all writers use language. Why is it so important to talk about it?**

> Each text has its own particular tone or mood – its own 'flavour'. It's the choice of language that creates this mood – and the drama. Looking closely at the language brings you closer to the meaning and the 'feeling' of the text.

FOUR WAYS LANGUAGE IS USED IN *MACBETH*

1 Repeated key words and phrases

Certain words and phrases appear again and again throughout the play. **Repetition** reinforces ideas and establishes a **mood**.

Examples: '*blood*', '*sleep*'.

How many references in the play can you find to **blood** and **sleep**?

2 Powerful adjectives and nouns

The use of **powerful adjectives** and nouns can provoke strong reactions from the audience.

Example: Macbeth's words on seeing the Witches again:
'*How now, you secret, black and midnight hags!*'
(Act 4 Scene 1)

3 Imagery: contrasts

Particularly strong descriptions create images in the audience's minds. Often, an image is made **stronger when contrasted** with something else.

Example: disease and health

Macbeth has a '*distempered cause*' (evil state), whilst Malcolm is the '*medicine*'.
(Act 5 Scene 2)

4 Imagery: metaphor and simile

Even stronger descriptions such as **similes and metaphors**, create images in the mind. Through such strong images, the audience can **see** and **feel** the meaning.

Example: Macbeth's words to Lady Macbeth
'*O, full of scorpions is my mind…!*'
(Act 3 Scene 2)

REPEATED KEY WORDS AND PHRASES

You have seen how many times the words '*blood*' and '*bloody*' are used in the play. This is an example of one key word that appears again and again.

Examples of '*blood*' in one short extract from Act 2 Scene 3

These examples are taken from the discovery of the murder until the point at which Malcolm and Donaldbain decide to leave.

Who refers to '*blood*'?	What do they say?
Macbeth telling Malcolm and Donaldbain that their father is dead.	'…the fountain of your **blood** / Is stopped.'
Lennox describing how the grooms had blood on them.	'Their hands and faces were all badged with **blood**, / So were their daggers.'
Macbeth justifying why he killed the grooms.	Here lay Duncan, / His silver skin laced with his golden **blood**…
Banquo saying everyone should meet to discuss what has happened.	'…let us meet / And question this most **bloody** piece of work / To know it further.'
Donaldbain, to his brother, warning him that even close friends may be the most dangerous.	'Where we are, / There's daggers in men's smiles; the nea'er in **blood**, / The nearer **bloody**.

So what does this use of language tell us about *Macbeth*?

The point is that this is a play about **murder** and **power**. **Blood** is repeated because it is **central to the play**. Think about it. *Macbeth* is a play about the **death** of **fathers**, **mothers** and **children**, and also explores the idea of **inheritance** and **family bloodlines**.

Remember

'*Blood*' and '*sleep*' are only two (though perhaps the most important) of the key words that run through Macbeth.

These words **provide tone, mood** and **drama**, but they also contribute to the themes Shakespeare is exploring throughout the play. We have already seen how 'sleep' reflects the theme of 'order and chaos' (see page 43).

2

POWERFUL ADJECTIVES AND NOUNS

Shakespeare uses a lot of powerful language. Looking at some of the stronger **adjectives** and **nouns** can help your understanding of the characters and the atmosphere of the play.

Example 1: Malcolm calls Macbeth a '*dead butcher*' and Lady Macbeth his '*fiend-like queen*' (Act 5 Scene 9)

What does this mean?   **Noun:**   *butcher* = someone who slaughters in cold-blood to 'feed' their appetite.
Adjective: *fiend-like* = the Devil was often referred to as 'the fiend' so this means 'devilish'.

Why is this important? Malcolm might want the *other* characters in the play to forget that Macbeth was once loyal, or that he was a brave fighter. Similarly, by associating Lady Macbeth with the devil, he ensures there is no pity or sympathy for her, despite the manner of her death. But you need to remember that these are Malcolm's words. Shakespeare may want us (the audience) to see Macbeth differently, Macbeth may have been murderous, but he was able to conquer his fears and remained a brave fighter to the last. Without the Witches he could have been a great man.

What do you think? How do you see Macbeth? What evidence can you find in the text to support your point of view?

I grant him bloody, Luxurious, avaricious, false, deceitful…

Example 2: Malcolm, Macbeth and Macduff

We can see the effect of **adjectives** and **nouns** in several things Malcolm says in **Act 4 Scene 3**.

Who Malcolm describes	What Malcolm says	The effect
Malcolm describes **Macbeth** to Macduff.	'*I grant him* **bloody**, / **Luxurious**, **avaricious**, **false**, **deceitful**, / **Sudden**, **malicious**…' (these are all adjectives)	In other words, he feels Macbeth is violent, greedy, mean, untrustworthy and enjoys causing harm. The fact that Malcolm uses such a long list of adjectives illustrates to the audience how strongly he feels about Macbeth. The words sum up the strength of feeling of those who oppose Macbeth. This is the first time Macbeth is described so openly.
Malcolm describes **Macduff** later in the scene, after Macduff has shown how much he cares for Scotland.	*Macduff, this* **noble passion**, / **Child of integrity**, *hath from my soul* / *Wiped the* **black scruples**, *reconciled my thoughts* / *To thy* **good truth** *and* **honour**.'	These descriptions contrast with the way Macbeth has been spoken about. Macduff's '*noble passion*' suggests he cares deeply and that he has royal blood in him. Macduff has integrity and has wiped away the doubts (*'scruples'*) that Malcolm had about him.

Example 3: Scotland's suffering, England's hope

Throughout Act 4 Scene 3, we also see Scotland described using adjectives and nouns. The two countries are described in very different language, highlighting the plight of Scotland. This has a simple, **dramatic impact on the audience**.

An example of how **Scotland** is described:

Speaker	Words	Effect
Ross (to Malcolm and Macduff)	*'Alas, **poor country** / …It cannot / Be called **our mother, but our grave**.'*	This conveys the idea that Scotland is in a very sorry state. The country no longer provides life and protection, but is a place in which all will die.

An example of how **England** is described:

Speaker	Words	Effect
Malcolm (to Macduff)	*'And here from **gracious England** have I offer / Of **goodly thousands**.'* (thousands of soldiers).	Here, *'gracious'* refers to King Edward, the angelic English King, and again shows the contrast between decent rulers and the 'tyrant' Macbeth.

Example 4: The language of the witches

The Witches' language is full of powerful **nouns** – things, creatures, objects, liquids.

In Act 4 Scene 1 the Witches list what is going into the cauldron:

'poisoned entrails' = inside of the stomach

'sweltered venom' = poisonous sweat

'ravined salt-sea shark' = full up with creatures it has eaten

'finger of birth-strangled babe' = finger of a child killed at birth

'fillet of fenny snake', 'eye of newt, 'toe of frog', 'lizard's leg'.

These are, for the most part, things that people in Shakespeare's time would have seen as evil or, at best, to be avoided.

> Fillet of a fenny snake,
> In the cauldron boil and bake:
> Eye of newt and toe of frog,
> Wool of bat and tongue of dog…

The effect?

These descriptions add to the strangely appealing, but poisonous setting Macbeth enters when he arrives a little later. The nouns conjure images and ideas in the mind of the audience that are all related to witchcraft and sorcery. This means that the audience is fully engaged with the atmosphere.

3

IMAGERY: CONTRASTS

Macbeth is a very visual play. Through the imagery Shakespeare uses, he 'paints pictures' in the audience's mind. The power of the play does not just come from the scenes you see on stage, but also from the images conjured in the mind by the language. Shakespeare sometimes creates these pictures through **contrasting** two things.

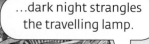

...dark night strangles the travelling lamp.

Example 1: Darkness and light

After the murder of Duncan, Ross and an Old Man meet outside the castle (Act 2 Scene 4). Ross describes how it is **unnaturally dark** considering it is daytime.

What Ross says	**When Ross could have said**

Act 2 Scene 4

*'By th'clock tis day
And yet dark night strangles the travelling lamp.'*

▶ 'It is actually daytime,
But it is really dark.'

Here, Shakespeare uses **personification**.
Personification means to give an object or a thing human qualities.

Ross *personifies* the dark night by saying it is 'strangling' the sun (the *'travelling lamp'*).
● *'Strangles'* is a very good word because it creates a murderous image in our mind.
● *'Travelling lamp'* is an image of the sun, like a lamp, moving across the sky, which is then smothered with darkness when it is 'strangled'.

There are several other references to **darkness** and **light** in the play:

Act 5 Scene 5

*'Out, out **brief candle**,
Life's but a **walking shadow**, a poor player
That struts and frets his **hour** upon the stage
And then is **heard no more**.'*

On hearing of his wife's death, Macbeth reflects on the **insignificance** of life, comparing it to a candle. Life = light.
The end of the 'play', in contrast, is silence and darkness (and death).

Act 3 Scene 2

*'Come, **seeling night**,
Scarf up the tender **eye** of pitiful **day**
And with thy bloody and invisible hand
Cancel and tear to pieces that great bond
Which keeps me **pale**…'*

Macbeth wants the night to come quickly, so the murder of Banquo can go ahead. Night and the sun are personified again: *'seeling'* means 'blinding'; *'the tender eye'* is the sun.

Act 1 Scene 4

*'Stars, hide your fires,
Let not light see my black and deep desires...'*

Macbeth asks for darkness to hide his murderous plans.

Example 2: Disease and health

Throughout the play we see the contrast of disease and health:

images of health and happiness = what is good and right

images of sickness and disease = what is evil and unjust

Lennox

In Act 2 Scene 3 Lennox, describing the night of the murder, says:

> Some say the earth was **feverous** and did shake.

This creates an image of the earth as almost human – uncomfortable with the crimes that are being committed by Macbeth.

Macbeth

In Act 4 Scene 1, Macbeth associates the Witches with disease:

> **Infected** be the air whereon they ride, And damned all those who trust them.

This also suggests that the Witches have infected Macbeth, leading to his damnation (being sent to hell). This is interesting, because later we hear Lady Macbeth's mind described as *'infected'* (by the Doctor, in Act 5 Scene 1).

In Act 5 Scene 4 Macbeth asks the Doctor if there is a special drug that can rid his country of the English army facing him.

> *'…what purgative drug Would scour these English hence?'*

Caithness

In Act 5 Scene 2 Caithness speaks of Macbeth:

> He cannot buckle his **distempered** cause…

…meaning, Macbeth cannot control his diseased kingdom.

But, in contrast, he describes Malcolm as:

> …the **med'cine** of the **sickly weal**,

He is the remedy, or cure, for the diseased country.

Malcolm

In Act 4 Scene 3 Malcolm says Scotland is like a wounded woman:

> It weeps, it **bleeds**, and each new day a **gash** Is added to **her wounds**.

4

IMAGERY: METAPHOR AND SIMILE

Shakespeare uses **metaphor** and **simile** to add even greater power to what characters say.

Remember that a **simile** is when you say that something is **like** something else; a **metaphor** is when you describe something by saying it **is** something else.

When Macbeth says in Act 3 Scene 2: *'O, full of scorpions is my mind, dear wife!'* we get a really strong image of the maddening thoughts in his head. This is important because it gives us an **insight** into the depth of his feelings.

Scorpions are creatures which sting and cause pain – they also provoke fear. By saying that he has scorpions in his mind, Macbeth is expressing the nature of the thoughts within his head. By describing his thoughts as scorpions, we can appreciate just how painful and frightening they are – we can really feel how troubled his mind is.

Other powerful metaphors used in the play

A heavy summons lies **like lead** upon me…

Banquo to Fleance, Act 2 Scene 1

Banquo says that thoughts and ideas are weighing heavily on his mind and he cannot sleep. Does he already suspect Macbeth of murder?

Now does he feel his title Hang loosely about him, **like a giant's robe Upon a dwarfish thief**.

Angus, about Macbeth, Act 5 Scene 2

Angus means that Macbeth now realises that he does not fit the role of king, having 'stolen' it from its rightful owner, Duncan.

We have **scorched the snake, not killed it**…

Macbeth, Act 3 Scene 2

Macbeth means that killing Duncan did not end things – unless he acts again, he will not be safe.

Life's but **a walking shadow**, a **poor player** That **struts and frets his hour upon the stage** And then is **heard no more**. It is **a tale Told by an idiot**, full of **sound and fury Signifying nothing**.

Macbeth, after he has heard about his wife's death, Act 5 Scene 5.

Macbeth compares life (his life and his wife's) to an actor's. It is not real, and has no meaning. They have had their 'sixty minutes of fame', but it has not brought them success or happiness, or even wisdom.

QUICK CHECK

How well do you understand Shakespeare's use of language? Find out using this quick test.

1. Name three unpleasant things that the Witches put into their cauldron.

2. When Macbeth says '*Out, out brief candle...*' is he referring to:
   (a) Life
   (b) The moon
   (c) The sun

3. Ross says that although it is daytime, night '*strangles*' the sun in Act 2 Scene 4.
   Why is this an appropriate image?
   (a) Because Duncan was strangled.
   (b) Because Duncan was murdered and this is a murderous image.
   (c) Because Duncan's son was strangled.

4. When Macbeth tells Malcolm and Donaldbain that the '*fountain of your blood is stopped...*'.
   Does he mean:
   (a) Their father is no longer bleeding.
   (b) They can stop crying now.
   (c) The father who made them and gave them blood is dead.

5. Who is '*bloody, luxurious, avaricious, false, deceitful, sudden and malicious...*'?
   (a) Macbeth
   (b) Lady Macbeth
   (c) The ghost of Banquo

6. What evidence is there in Act 4 Scene 3 that Scotland is like an injured or sick person?

Think microscopes!

do brilliantly!

Higher levels are gained in the Test by those students who really **study and explore words and phrases in detail**.
For example, in Macbeth's famous 'brief candle' speech in Act 5, he compares his own life to that of an actor (a '*poor player*') in a meaningless play.

By putting this language **under the microscope**, let's see what can be learned.

- If Macbeth's life is a 'play' – who is the director? Who is responsible for what happens to Macbeth? It could be that Macbeth **cannot face** what he has done and **he alone is responsible**.

- Perhaps the Witches direct what happens? What about their apparent promises?

- Or, it could be that Macbeth is reminding us that the real director of our lives is God and however much we shout, and fight for what we want, **God will decide our fate**.

1 Understanding the question

'Understanding the question' sounds easy enough, doesn't it? However, in the Test, you have to be especially careful that you understand **exactly what you have to do**. If you do not, you will not be answering the question and your mark will be low.

What do I have to do in the Test?

You have to produce a continuous piece of writing on *Macbeth* for the Shakespeare section of the Test. This means you have to write on **two scenes** from the play. The question will link these two scenes together and you must **write about both scenes** in your answer.

For example:

> **Macbeth**
>
> Act 2 Scene 1
> Act 3 Scene 1
>
> **What different impressions do we get
> of Banquo in these two extracts?**

What is this question asking?

You will find that it is a lot easier to understand what a question is asking you to do if you break it down first.

You may already have your own way of breaking down a question, but the following process is good practice for the Test.

Key words	Conclusions	Action
Highlight the key words from the question. In this case: ● 'What' ● 'different impressions' ● 'we' ● 'Banquo' ● 'two extracts'.	From these key words we can conclude: ● The word 'what' and the named character tell us this is a question about character and behaviour (Banquo's) and how it comes across to the audience ('we'). ● It is also suggesting that Banquo is 'different' in the two extracts. This difference could be: in his behaviour/ actions, or in his relationship to other characters (e.g. Macbeth).	What you do with these conclusions in the Test: ● Write about Banquo mainly – what impression we get. ● Write about other characters only in their relationship to Banquo. ● Look at how he is different in the two scenes or how he changes/ develops.

What will the Test question be about?

In the Test, the question will target one of the following areas:

- ► Character and motivation
- ► Ideas, themes and issues
- ► The language of the text
- ► The text in performance

The sample question on page 58 targets **Character and motivation**. The question looks at Banquo's **character**. **How** it changes (the different impressions) is related to **motivation** – why he acts as he does.

Here are two more examples of Test questions:

1

Act 2 Scene 4
(Old Man and Ross outside Macbeth's castle)
Act 3 Scene 4
(Banquet scene with Banquo's ghost)

How is the **idea of order and chaos/disorder presented** in these **two extracts**?

- 'How' suggests the way something occurs or is shown.
- 'presented' tells us we must look for what Shakespeare shows us in these scenes.
- 'idea' is a word often used to mean theme. The theme here is order and chaos, so this is a question about how this theme appears.
- You will need to find evidence of it in the two extracts.

2

Act 2 Scene 3
(The discovery of Duncan's murder)
Act 4 Scene 3
(Malcolm's meeting with Macduff)

How do **characters** use **language** to **hide what they really feel** in these **two extracts**?

- 'How' suggests the way something occurs or is shown.
- The question mentions 'characters' so this is not about any one person in these scenes.
- The word 'language', tells us this is the focus – and that you will need to read beneath the surface of the actual words to get at what the characters' actual feelings are, and their reasons for hiding them.
- You will need to find evidence in the two extracts.

TIP

Some questions, like Question 2, above, can cover **more than one area**. For example, Malcolm pretends to be a bad person in Act 4 Scene 3 in order to test Macduff's loyalty. This is the **main point** you would make. Of course, this also **shows** us Malcolm is a clever and cunning leader. **But** beware, this is **not the main point** you would make.

Remember that the question is about **how** the characters **use language**; it is not about Malcolm himself. Be careful that you do not 'go off the point' of the question.

QUICK CHECK

Look at the question below.

Act 1 Scene 3 and
Act 4 Scene 1

What different impressions do we get of the Witches in these two scenes?

- Which of the four skill areas is this question looking at (**character and motivation; ideas, themes and issues; the language of the text; the text in performance**)?
- Highlight the key words and decide what the question is asking you to do and what you would include in your answer.

2 Finding and using evidence

Evidence is one thing that you **must never forget** when writing about *Macbeth*, or any text. **Without evidence**, you have **no proof** for the things you say and your answer is really not worth very much. Using evidence in your answer means that you quote from the text and refer to the text in order to support the points that you make.

Finding evidence for your answer

Let's look again at the sample Test question used in the last unit and see **how** you go about finding the quotes you need.

The table below contains the evidence about **Banquo** that you can find in **Act 2 Scene 1**.

> Act 2 Scene 1
> Act 3 Scene 1
>
> **What different impressions do we get of Banquo in these two extracts?**

Focus	Evidence	Impressions given
How Banquo acts	Banquo draws his sword.	Banquo is **jumpy** – he feels that there is **murder in the air**.
What Banquo says	Banquo says he feels a heaviness on him: '*A heavy summons lies like lead upon me...*' and that he cannot sleep.	Banquo is very **uneasy** – perhaps **anxious** about Macbeth's plans and the Witches' prophecies.
	He also refuses to say one way or the other whether he will support Macbeth in the future.	This suggests Banquo **has his own plans** and he is thinking about what the Witches have promised him. This could also give the impression that he, too, is **ambitious**.
How others act towards him	Macbeth asks Banquo to support him: '*If you shall cleave to my consent, when 'tis, / It shall make honour for you.*'	Macbeth is testing Banquo – but Banquo's response **creates tension** between them.
What others say	Fleance talks about the night: '*The moon is down...*'	Fleance talks in a simple, yet close way with his father. This shows the **solidarity** between them.

Remember

You are looking at **two** scenes and **comparing the different impressions** of Banquo, so do not spend all your time looking only at one scene. This would be an incomplete answer and will only ever get you a maximum of half marks!

> ...but still keep My bosom franchised and allegiance clear, ...

Let's look at what evidence there is about Banquo in the second scene: **Act 3 Scene 1**.

Focus	Evidence	Impressions given
How Banquo acts	▶ Banquo is dressed for riding; he speaks his thoughts to the audience, but keeps quiet when people approach.	▶ Perhaps Banquo is **keen to get away** from the castle? He has his own thoughts and ideas – this is the first time we see him speak alone.
What Banquo says	▶ Banquo says about Macbeth: *'I fear / Thou played'st most foully for it...'*	▶ This shows that Banquo is pretty **certain** that **Macbeth was responsible** for Duncan's murder.
	▶ Banquo says about the Witches: *'May they not be my oracles as well / And set me up in hope?'*	▶ Here Banquo **dwells upon** what the **Witches said** to him and takes hope from it. Could it be that he is as **taken in** by what they say as Macbeth?
How others act towards him	▶ Macbeth seeks information about Banquo's movements.	▶ Banquo is a man who is **under threat**, but may not realise it. Perhaps he thinks the Witches' promises will keep him safe?
What others say	▶ Macbeth both praises and scorns Banquo: *'...his royalty of nature'* and *'dauntless temper...'* Macbeth says it is Banquo's fault that he killed Duncan – so that Banquo's children could become kings.	▶ Through hearing Macbeth's thoughts, Banquo is made to seem **more noble** and **our impression of him is enhanced**, especially when contrasted with Macbeth and his plans.

TIP

Remember that it is **very bad style** just to list quotes in your writing. The evidence (quotes) needs to be a part of your writing and not just 'stuck in' because you have been told that you need to quote!

Point, Evidence, Explanation

This formula is very useful to remember:

- **P**oint: Make a statement.
- **E**vidence: Quote your evidence from the text to support your point.
- **E**xplanation: Expand on your point with reference to the evidence you have used.

This is a **fool-proof way of making sure that you use evidence correctly**.

Using evidence in your answer

You need to be careful that the evidence you select is **useful** and **valid** for the question you are answering. In the question on page 60 you are being asked to discuss the **impressions of Banquo**, not Fleance or Macbeth. **Any reference to these characters needs to be in relation to Banquo** and the impression we get of him.

There are different ways of using evidence. You do not **always** need to quote the text directly. Sometimes you can **paraphrase** or **summarise** what a character says to show what he/she is feeling/thinking. Here are two ways of expressing the same information.

Paraphrasing and summarising

Paraphrasing or **summarising** means stating what has happened or what a character has said, felt, or shown in **your own words**.

Example:

> Banquo fails to offer support to Macbeth when he is asked for it, saying he'd rather remain his own person for the time being.

Direct quotation

A **direct quotation** means putting into your answer the **exact words** said by a character.

Example:

> Banquo tells Macbeth that he'll keep his 'allegiance clear...' By 'allegiance' he means his loyalty to one group.

Here, '*allegiance clear...*' are **the actual words from the play** (said by Banquo in Act 2 Scene 1). Note that they have been put into inverted commas/speech marks to show that these are **not** the student's words.

There is more on both **paraphrasing** and **using direct quotations** in the next unit on pages 64–67.

QUICK CHECK

There are **four** pointers used in the tables on pages 60 and 61:

1. how a character behaves
2. what they say
3. how others act towards them
4. what others say.

Take **any one** of these pointers, and make a note of the impression the evidence gives of Lady Macbeth in Act 5 Scene 1. Use both skill areas (paraphrasing and direct quotation) when using evidence in your answer.

Levels of evidence

Sticking to the **P.E.E. rule** is a good way to make sure that you use evidence correctly. However, you should consider the **level guide** below so that you use evidence in the best way possible for **maximum marks**.

Lower level evidence

You will get a lower Test level if:

- **you do not provide any evidence** for your opinion at all

- you include quotations but just **copy** them and **do not offer a reason** for including them.

> Banquo is cautious about the witches in the first scene.

> This essay is about Banquo. He tells Macbeth that 'to win us to our harm/The instruments of darkness tell us truths...'.

Medium level evidence

You will only get a medium level if:

- you include quotations – in support of what you say – but do not really develop your ideas (expansion). You might pick on a key line or dialogue but only say something very basic and obvious about it.

> In this scene, Banquo says the witches might be evil. He tells Macbeth that 'to win us to our harm/The instruments of darkness tell us truths...'.

Higher level evidence

To get the highest levels:

- the evidence you select needs to be **relevant and really support what you want to say.**

- you take the evidence you have mentioned and either **link it to supporting evidence, or use it to contrast** with **other points** you are making.

- you provide **further explanation** or **offer possibilities** as a result of the evidence.

do brilliantly !

> The impression given of Banquo in Act 1 Scene 3 is of a man who, though interested in the witches, already suspects their motives. As he says to Macbeth 'to win us to our harm/The instruments of darkness tell us truths...'
>
> By Act 2 Scene 1, this same man gives the impression of someone not simply anxious about the forces of darkness but unable to sleep or rest easy. He tells Fleance that 'a heavy summons lies like lead' on him.
>
> Does he know, deep in his heart what Macbeth is about to do? He certainly give that impression when he draws his sword when Macbeth enters.

3 Paraphrasing, summarising

As mentioned in Unit 2, you can **paraphrase**, **summarise** or **use quotes** when you are writing the points you use as evidence.

Imagine you have been asked this question in the Test:

> Act 1 Scene 6
> Act 2 Scene 3
>
> **How is the theme of appearance and reality developed in these two scenes?**

How to paraphrase the dialogue

Using Act 1 Scene 6 as an example, one way of making your points is to **paraphrase** what is said. This means putting actual lines and details from the play into your own words.

Here are some examples of **good paraphrasing**. Note how the good paraphrase finds a **different way** of saying the information, but it keeps the **tone** of the original quote.

The facts and the dialogue Act 1 Scene 6	Paraphrase
Duncan, Banquo and the Thanes arrive outside Macbeth's castle Duncan: *'This castle hath a pleasant seat; the air / Nimbly and sweetly recommends itself…'*	▶ As the King and his court prepare to enter the castle, **he comments on how agreeable the setting is.**
Banquo: *'The temple-haunting martlet, does approve / By his loved mansionry that the heaven's breath / Smells wooingly here.'*	▶ Banquo points out a bird — a martlet — normally **found in sacred places,** and how this adds to **the fragrant welcome** of the castle.
Lady Macbeth greets them Lady Macbeth: *'All our service, / In every point twice done and then done double, / Were poor and single business to contend / Against those honours deep and broad wherewith / Your majesty loads our house.'*	▶ As Lady Macbeth greets her guests she says how **even if she and Macbeth had multiplied all they had done** for the King, it would not have compared with the great rewards he has granted them.

and using quotations

In order to paraphrase effectively you need to:

1 **Know the facts**
Be clear about **what is going on** so you can put the action and ideas into your own words.

In the examples of paraphrasing in the table on page 64, it is clear that:
- Duncan and Banquo are praising the heavenly qualities of Macbeth's castle
- Lady Macbeth is being especially welcoming in order to hide what she has planned.

2 **Find words that are close in meaning (and tone) to the original text**
Here are some of the alternative words found by the student in the example on page 64.

Original words or phrases	Paraphrase
'...castle hath a *pleasant seat*' '...*temple-haunting* martlet' '...those *honours deep* and *broad*...'	pleasant = agreeable; seat = setting ...found in sacred places ('*temple*') ...great rewards...

How to summarise the action

Examiners **do not** want to see you simply re-telling the story of *Macbeth*. If you have to summarise, do so in **clear, fluent** explanations.

Low level summary

The whole explanation is **too long**. If you are going to summarise what happens **make it short**! For example, **all the names are mentioned** unnecessarily.

'place' is **too general** – use the name of the castle (Dunsinane) or 'castle'.

Too chatty and informal. This doesn't really give the sense of how Lady Macbeth is falsely flattering the King.

> King Duncan, Macduff, Banquo and all the other Thanes and the King's servants come to Macbeth and Lady Macbeth's **place** in Act 1 Scene 6. They are met by Lady Macbeth who talks in a posh, but **unreal way** about how she is **really glad** to have the King there and says it's **so nice** that the King has given them all these special **things**.

Higher level summary

This is a **single paragraph summary**. Precise and to the point.

The word 'court' sums up who is there.

'Dunsinane' is better than 'place'.

This neat phrase sums up Lady Macbeth's behaviour.

'Honours' tells us that the King has rewarded and valued Macbeth.

do brilliantly !

> Duncan, Banquo and his court arrive at **Dunsinane** where Lady Macbeth greets them with a **pretence of courtesy and gratitude** for the honours the King has granted Macbeth.

How to use quotations

A quotation is when you include the exact words said by a character in the play in order to make a point. It is important that you quote **regularly** and **relevantly** in your Test answer. Also, remember that **you must ALWAYS use speech marks when you quote from a text**.

Look at this sample Test question:

> Act 2 Scene 3
> Act 4 Scene 3
>
> **How does Shakespeare use language to show the contrast between good and evil in these two scenes?**

TIP

Do not forget
P. E. E.:

Point, **E**vidence, **E**xplanation.

Now look at a section from one student's answer. Look at *how* the quotation has been used and placed in the student's answer.

The student makes the point about religious/holy language.

A **direct quotation** from Macduff is used as evidence of this language.

An **explanation** is made about the quotation.

> Religious language is used by Macduff when he describes how 'most **sacrilegious** murder hath broke ope the **Lord's anointed temple**' (Act 2 Scene 3) after he has discovered Duncan's body. This links Duncan's murder to a crime against God.

Note that the **original quotation** (which comes from Act 2 Scene 3 after Macduff has found Duncan murdered) was as follows:

Macduff:	*Confusion now hath made his masterpiece:*
	Most sacrilegious murder hath broke ope
	The Lord's anointed temple *and stole thence*
	The life o' th' building.

This is the quotation that the student chose to include to support the point being made.

In simple terms, the structure of the student's comments looks like this:

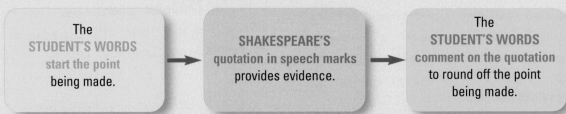

| The **STUDENT'S WORDS** start the point being made. | → | **SHAKESPEARE'S** quotation in speech marks provides evidence. | → | The **STUDENT'S WORDS** comment on the quotation to round off the point being made. |

Other ways of using quotations

Lists of linked words

Sometimes, rather than quoting a whole line, or part of a line, you might want to focus on individual words. Look at this example, answering the same question as on page 66.

> In Act 4 Scene 3 Shakespeare uses language to paint a clear picture of Macbeth's evil nature, with characters calling him, at various points in the scene, a 'tyrant', 'treacherous', 'black', 'devilish', and 'bloody-sceptered...'

Note how the student puts each individual word or phrase into separate sets of inverted commas to reflect the fact that these are said at different times in different speeches in the scene.

Putting the quoted words together like this gives really clear evidence of the point being made.

Longer quotations

Try to avoid these, unless you are able to comment on the whole section you have included. If not, the Test marker may assume you are simply trying to fill the page.

Here is a good example from the same answer.

do **brilliantly** !

> In Act 4 Scene 3 Malcolm makes Macbeth's evil nature especially clear when he says:
>
> 'I grant him bloody,
> Luxurious, avaricious, false, deceitful,
> Sudden, malicious, smacking of every sin
> That has a name.'
>
> This is a real catalogue of evil as it describes Macbeth as liking bloodshed, being greedy, treacherous, and spiteful in the extreme. It ends by saying that he embodies every possible human fault and crime.

The point is made by the student.

The quotation is placed apart as it is a longer one.

A comment on what is meant by the quotation follows.

QUICK CHECK

Here is a line said by the doctor about Lady Macbeth when she is sleep-walking in Act 5 Scene 1:
'What a sigh is there? The heart is sorely charged.'

Put part of this quotation into a statement about Lady Macbeth's behaviour in this scene. Start with: We can see that Lady Macbeth...

4 Structuring your answer

The **structure** is the **order** and the **sequence** that you use when you write your answer. The structure is not **what** you say (i.e. the themes and ideas) but **how** you put your ideas across – the argument you develop.

You need to think about **how** you answer a Test question **before** you begin writing. Think about it this way: you want to make a cake, and you may know how you want the cake to taste, but if you do not follow the recipe, and add the ingredients in the right order, you may not end up with a cake at all, you may end up with a complete mess! It is the same with writing essays. So, always **think structure, or your argument may fall apart!**

Look at these two fairly typical Test questions:

> Act 4 Scene 3 and
> Act 5 Scene 9 (the last scene of the play)
>
> **What impression do we get of Malcolm in these two extracts?**

> Act 1 Scene 1 and
> Act 5 Scene 1
>
> **How is the theme of chaos and disorder developed in these two extracts?**

> What approach am I going to take in order to answer this question in the best way?

There are **two** ways you can approach answering such questions:

Approach 1

Write about **each scene in turn** in relation to the **subject** of the question.

Structure
- Introduction
- First scene – points
- Second scene – points
- Conclusion

Advantages
- Easy-to-follow
- Clear and straightforward to read

Disadvantages
- You might end up just retelling what happened and not analysing.
- It can be difficult to link ideas and draw comparisons with this approach.

Approach 2

Take the **subject** of the question and write about **each point in turn** in relation to each scene.

Structure
- Introduction
- First point – relevant to each scene
- Second point – relevant to each scene
- Third point – relevant to each scene
- Conclusion

Advantages
- Possibly more interesting
- Less danger of just retelling the story

Disadvantages
- More complicated
- Jumping between scenes can be difficult.

How do I use these structures in my writing?

Take a look at the first question on page 68 (the impression we get of Malcolm in the two scenes). This is how you would answer this question using both approaches.

Approach 1

Using this approach, you would **deal with each scene in turn**. You would discuss all the impressions of Malcolm in the first scene before moving on to discuss the impressions we get of him in the second scene.

Act 4 Scene 3
- Clever
- Cautious
- Persuasive

Act 5 Scene 9
- Clever
- Compassionate
- Persuasive

Finally, you would conclude your answer by making comparisons between the impressions of Malcolm in the two scenes and commenting on any differences or similarities.

Approach 2

With this approach, you **deal with each point in turn**. You would discuss a point in relation to both Scene 3 and 9 before moving on to the next point and doing the same with that.

- **His cleverness** – you would write about how this is shown in **both scenes**.
- **His persuasiveness** – how this is shown in **both scenes**.
- **His caution** – you would write about how this is shown in the **first** scene, but **not the second**.
- **His compassion** – you would write about how this is shown **only in the second scene**.
- You would **conclude** in a similar way to Approach 1 – by making comparisons and commenting on differences and similarities between the impressions of Malcolm in the two scenes.

Which approach (1 or 2) do you think the following student is using?

do brilliantly!

One of the impressions we get of Malcolm is how persuasive he is. For example in Act 4 Scene 3 he persuades Macduff to put aside his despair over the death of his family, and turn it into anger. He tells him: 'let grief convert to anger...' and this spurs Macduff on.

We also see this persuasiveness in Act 5 Scene 9 when Malcolm tells the Thanes that he has made them all Earls. This is used to persuade them to remain loyal by showing them they will be rewarded. It is a different kind of persuasion to that shown in Act 4 Scene 3 because it is almost buying their loyalty, whereas with Macduff he had appealed to his emotions.

This is a **successful answer** because:

- it integrates quotation
- it compares one aspect of his character across two scenes
- it reveals differences between the types of persuasion he uses in the two scenes.

Have a look through the answer again and see if you can spot all these elements.

How to use paragraphs and sentences to organise your ideas

How can I grab the attention of the examiner? I want him to notice my work!

Whichever approach you use, a well-structured paragraph can make the points you wish to make crystal clear. Remember, it is not just the **overall structure** that is important, you also need to consider carefully the structure of **each paragraph**.

For good paragraph structure you can use the topic sentence (often the first sentence of a paragraph) to make the main point. As you see in this example, you then expand upon the topic sentence, using evidence, in the rest of the paragraph.

The first sentence here gets the key point across. This is why it is called the topic sentence. It uses a word from the question title ('impression') and then says what that impression of Malcolm is (he is persuasive).

The second sentence provides the evidence to support the main point made in the first sentence. It is in this sentence that the student expands on the key point.

> One of the impressions we get of Malcolm is how persuasive he is. For example, in Act 4 Scene 3 he persuades Macduff to put aside his despair over the death of his family, and turn it into anger.

 TIP

Style is also essential when writing an answer to a Test question. It is important that you use interesting **connectives** when linking ideas together. In the student's answer above, the phrase 'For example,' **links (or connects)** the **topic sentence** (the main point) and the **evidence**. To make your writing interesting try to vary the way you link points and evidence together.

Instead of using 'for example' you could try:
- 'This can be seen when...' or 'This is shown in...' or 'We see this in...'

Higher level sentences

 do brilliantly!

To get a higher mark, you need to attract the Test marker's attention. Try constructing paragraphs in more imaginative ways. Make interesting and valid points about the text. Remember, the Test marker will have read hundreds of answers – make yours stand out.

Look at this example.

> Clever, cautious and persuasive are three words we can use to sum up the impression we get of Malcolm in Act 4 Scene 3, but what evidence is there for this?

Note the **structure of the sentence**: starting a paragraph with a **pattern of three adjectives** is very memorable. This is not a style that basic answers would use.

The **rhetorical question** at the end of the paragraph is impressive. Why? Because *you* are going to answer your own question. It is like a trailer for your answer, it gives a clue about what you are going to say, it opens the debate.

Structuring your answer – a summary

In order to answer the question successfully you need to:

- **answer** what **the question** asks
- **support** what you write with **evidence**
- **structure** your answer in a **clear** and **logical** way
- **use a variety of connectives**
- **vary** your use of **sentence structure** so that your answer is memorable.

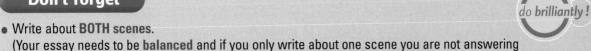

Don't forget

do brilliantly!

- Write about **BOTH scenes**.
  (Your essay needs to be **balanced** and if you only write about one scene you are not answering the question. Many students fall down here and their marks suffer as a result.)
- **Time yourself** so that you have enough time to write all your points on both scenes.
- **Leave about half the time** for the second scene if you are following **Approach 1**.
- **Divide your time equally** over your individual points, if you are following **Approach 2**.
- **Do not rush any section**, plan your time.
  (It is natural that **you might have more to say about one scene** than another, so the amount you write **need not be identical**.)
- **Focus your attention where it is needed** so you do not spend too long on one point but **balance the focus of the discussion**.
- **Do not** refer to **other scenes** or elements in the play **unless** it is helping you to make a point about the scenes you have been given. If you do not explain **why** you have referred to another scene and **why it is relevant to the question**, it is just useless information. You need to **link** the reference to the question.

For example: You might want to make the point that, in Act 2 Scene 3, Malcolm was a frightened young man fleeing for his life. This is **not relevant** to the question you have been asked, **unless** you point out that when we next see Malcolm (i.e. in Act 4 Scene 3) he has become an astute and clever man.

The plan

To help you avoid missing out anything important, you need to allow yourself **5 minutes from the 45 you are given** to plan your answer. **This is essential.**

Try to write down words and phrases as prompts and then put them into a logical order. Decide on the order **before** you begin writing – you may find it helps to number the paragraphs.

When you have a plan to follow, you can decide how long you need to spend on each section – and stick to it! You need to make timing yourself to write Test answers a part of your Test practice.

Intro   para 1
Act 4 Scene 3
cautious   para 2
persuasive   para 3
clever   para 4
Act 5 Scene 9
persuasive   5
clever   6
caring/compassionate   7
Conclusion   8

QUICK CHECK

In three minutes, try to write down adjectives (up to six in total) to describe Lady Macbeth in Act 1 Scene 7 and Act 5 Scene 1. Then write paragraph numbers next to each one to decide which order/priority you would use them to write about her.

Writing about two scenes

I MUST plan, but how?

In this section, we are going to look at how to go about putting together all the ideas you have within a time limit.

You know that in the Test you will have to answer on **two scenes** and, as we saw in Unit 4, the most straightforward way to do this is to **write about each scene in turn**. However, to get **maximum marks you must plan your answer**.

Planning the points

Here is an expanded plan of some points a student wants to make in answer to a question about the **impressions we get of Malcolm in Act 4 Scene 3, and in the final scene (Act 5 Scene 9)**. Practising with this format will help you to prepare a more concise plan for the Test.

Introductory paragraph: basic action/background

- **Act 4 Scene 3** – Malcolm meets with Macduff in England.
- **Act 5 Scene 9** – final scene: end of battle – Malcolm has just removed Macbeth and is now King.

Section on Act 4 Scene 3: points in order of importance

Impressions of Malcolm

- **Clever and cautious** – Malcolm has learned not to trust people after his father's murder. He says to Macduff '*What you have spoke, it may be so perchance.*' (i.e. what Macduff says he feels might be true).
- **Persuasive** – when Macduff finds out his family has been murdered, Malcolm persuades him to turn his despair to anger against Macbeth ('*let grief / convert to anger...*').

Section on Act 5 Scene 9: points in order of importance

Impressions of Malcolm

- **Compassionate** – Malcolm says that Siward's dead son is worth more than a few words from his father ('*He's worth more sorrow / and that I'll spend for him...*').
- **Clever** – he rewards the people who have fought with him by making them Earls, and emphasises the evil that he has replaced (Malcolm calls Macbeth a '*butcher*' and Lady Macbeth, '*fiend-like*').

Conclusion

Malcolm **grows from being a frightened son**, fleeing for his life, to the man we see in Act 4 Scene 3 who has learned to be cautious. By the end of the play, we get the impression **he will be a just king**, rewarding loyalty and be more alert and informed than his father.

Planning an essay in this way gives you a solid structure in which to make your points, but you need also to take care about **how** you express yourself. Your paragraphs need to be joined together logically, as do the ideas within each paragraph, otherwise your answer will not 'flow'.

Linking ideas within and between paragraphs

It is absolutely vital that you use connecting words and phrases to organise your writing. Learn what each of these **key connectives** means, and use them to make your points crystal clear.

Key connectives	Purpose	Meaning	Example
Firstly Then Secondly Later Finally	For sequence	To show the order in which events or processes occurred.	*Firstly, Malcolm tests Macduff, then when he is sure of his loyalty he reveals his true feelings.*
In the same way Similarly Also too Likewise	For comparison	To show similarities between ideas.	*In the same way that Duncan is described in a saintly way, so too Malcolm calls upon the 'grace of Grace' to help him rule.*
Moreover What is more In addition Exactly	For development or emphasis	To make a further point to support an idea.	*Moreover, Malcolm benefits from his father being seen in this way — as God's chosen ruler.*
On the other hand In contrast However But	For contrast	To show differences between ideas.	*In contrast to Act 4 Scene 3, in the final scene, Malcolm is now sure of himself.*
On the whole In conclusion To conclude Finally Overall To sum up Ultimately	For conclusion	To summarise and reflect on what has been written or discussed.	*Ultimately, at the end of the play, Malcolm shows himself to be a ruler who will have his finger on the pulse of what's going on.*

TIP

For a higher level in the Test you are required to explain and develop your ideas fully. You need to **demonstrate** that you are expanding on a point. If you use phrases such as 'What is more' and 'In addition' you are making it obvious to the marker that you have taken an idea and developed it.

Model answer

Looking at a model answer is a good way to improve your own skills. If you study the following response – break down the information, look to see **what** the student has done and **how** it has been done – you will find it much easier to be in control of your own writing.

This example deals with the **first** part of the answer, which contains:

- the **introductory paragraph**
- the first section in **Act 4 Scene 3**.

Opening paragraph sets the scene

> The two scenes deal with two key moments in the play. The first brings together Malcolm and Macduff in England, whilst the second gives us Malcolm as the new king, having displaced Macbeth.

First, a point about Malcolm

> The main impression we get of Malcolm in Act 4 Scene 3 is of a man who has learned to be **cautious** and **clever**. Let's not forget that he has seen his father murdered by a trusted Thane, and has himself been blamed. So, he naturally wants to test Macduff's loyalty, which is why when Macduff appeals to him for help, he replies,

Supporting quotation

> 'What you have spoke, it may be so perchance.'

Explanation and development

> In other words, he can't be sure Macduff hasn't been sent to trick Malcolm into returning to Scotland to be murdered. Malcolm therefore **goes on to say** that he is even worse than Macbeth, and that he wouldn't make a good king: 'better Macbeth, than such a one to reign.'

Summary of sequence of events

> So, **firstly** we have seen Malcolm test Macduff, **then** when he is sure of his loyalty, he reveals his true feelings.

Connective of time links to next point

> **Later** in the scene we see Malcolm's **persuasiveness**. When Macduff is told of the slaughter of his family, Malcolm is able to persuade Macduff to turn his despair to anger. He tells him, to '**let grief convert to anger**...'.

Supporting quotation

TIP

When the question asks about 'impressions of a character' **use the word 'impression' in your answer**.

For example, 'the impression we get is...'

This will help you to **stick to the point**. Also, it is likely that these impressions will be **adjectives**:

He is compassionate, clever, persuasive etc.

This example deals with the **second** part of the answer, which contains:

- **Act 5 Scene 9**
- The **conclusion**.

do brilliantly !

This paragraph shows how Malcolm is different in this scene

Act 5 Scene 9 presents Malcolm in a different way. In contrast to Act 4 Scene 3 he **now** seems sure of himself. The impression we get is of someone who is able now to show **compassion** (which he didn't really do when he heard of Macduff's family's murder). When old Siward reacts to his son's death with a few, brief words, Malcolm says that 'he's worth more in sorrow, and that I'll spend for him...'.

Supporting quotation

This point links back to the previous scene

However, he hasn't lost the **cleverness** he displayed **in Act 4 Scene 3**. He rewards the Thanes who fought with him by making them Earls, and emphasises the evil that he has replaced. He does this by calling Macbeth a '**butcher**' and Lady Macbeth, '**fiend-like**'.

More quotations

This is very important because he wants to create the impression that he, like his father, is rightfully king and chosen by God. **In the same way**, that Duncan was described in a saintly way, so too Malcolm calls upon the 'grace of Grace' to help him rule. This is a direct appeal to God.

Comparison drawn

Summing up connective

On the whole, the impression given of Malcolm **in these two scenes** is of someone who will be a ruler with his finger on the pulse of what's going on. He has **shown in the first scene that he is no fool**, and can be persuasive when he needs to be. **In the second scene he shows other qualities**, such as compassion, but also demonstrates how to keep himself in power.

Conclusion brings together the earlier points

QUICK CHECK

Here is a typical Test question:

> Act 1 Scene 5
> Act 4 Scene 2
>
> **How does Shakespeare explore the idea of good and evil in these two scenes?**

- Write the **opening paragraph** for this essay. Give a *very brief* summary of what happens (no more than 40 words).
- Write the **second paragraph**, dealing with Act 1 Scene 5. Make **one point** about evil in this scene, and **support it with a quotation**. Use **connectives** to link what you say.

What makes a top answer

However well you know the play, it is vital you understand what it takes to get **really high marks** in the Test. There are specific features that examiners are looking for and if you do not meet the criteria, you won't get the level. So, a good way to get top marks is to **know exactly what they are looking for**.

Every time I get the same level! What can I do to move up?

Features of Test levels

The following are broad guides only but they should give you a good idea of the sorts of things Test markers are looking for.

Lower level answers: level 4

- The student tends to **re-tell the plot** or events rather than comment.
- There are **irrelevant comments or information** (nothing to do with the question).
- The ideas are **poorly-expressed** using lazy or informal language.
- **Quotations** (if included) are copied out **without any real link** to the comments.
- Ideas **lack detail** and are undeveloped.
- One scene is sometimes **ignored**.

Medium level answers: level 5 to low level 6

- There is **more comment and analysis** of the scenes but **not always well-expressed**.
- There is some **development of ideas**, but it only goes so far.
- There is **an attempt to link evidence** (like quotations) **to points** made but it is done rather clumsily.
- **Some detail** on specific points is included; others are still dealt with rather too simply.

Higher level answers: high level 6 to level 7

- There is **wide comment** and **analysis** covering a **range of ideas**.
- Ideas are **fully developed**.
- There are suggestions of **other possibilities**, rather than one answer only.
- There is a clear **focus on details** and their relevance to the question.
- The points made show **insight** (looking beyond the obvious).
- **Evidence** is skilfully **woven into the writing**.

TIP

No marker expects you to write down every single thing you know about a scene. It is far better to explore two or three key points in detail with relevant quotations, than write down everything without any detailed comment or insight.

How to turn your level 4/5 answer into a level 6/7 answer

Here a student has written about the impressions we get of Macbeth in **Act 2 Scene 3** after the murder is discovered. This is just part of the answer.

Good start mentioning the impressions we get of Macbeth, but rather poorly-expressed: '*in this bit*'.

Tries to support the point with a quotation but not really the best choice. Better to use the one where he explains how devastated he felt at Duncan's death.

Explanation here, but more needed.

Tries to link a comment on Macbeth to Lady Macbeth's behaviour. Could do with evidence – why does she faint *at this point* exactly?

The last part seems to be more about telling us what happened. Where is the comment? Does this show he is ready to take control?

> Macbeth **seems able to hide his feelings** here and is a really great actor **in this bit** because he is able to pretend that he is upset by the King's death.
>
> > '...I do repent me of my fury
> > That I did kill them.'
>
> Macbeth says this about the servants he killed saying he's sorry for what he did. He killed them so they couldn't be questioned. This is pretty evil!
>
> But **he can't be that good an actor because Lady Macbeth has to pretend to faint** to stop people looking at him. So he's not really in control, is he?
>
> Then **he organises everyone later** and arranges that they should all meet in the hall together and think about what has happened. Then Malcolm and Donaldbain leave. They are very suspicious, so perhaps Macbeth acted suspiciously?

Marker's comment

This response:

- does attempt to talk about the impressions we get of Macbeth, but does so rather clumsily
- has too much retelling of events – Lady Macbeth's fainting, the killing of the servants, the arrangement to meet in the hall
- hasn't enough explanation of what this tells us about Macbeth
- refers to the servants' killing as being 'pretty evil' but it should be made clearer that this is an impression we get of Macbeth
- uses a supporting quotation but one that doesn't especially help us to understand Macbeth – and it is put in the answer rather suddenly
- has a good last point about Malcolm and Donaldbain but it is undeveloped.

This is a just about a **level 5**, but only just.

Moving this response up a level

do *brilliantly* !

Now look at part of the same answer, rewritten to include the things the marker has indicated needed to be improved or altered. The new text is in orange.

The word 'impression' is used from the start to make sure the answer is relevant.

Ideas are linked together using simple link phrases, such as 'for example'.

The chosen quotation is relevant as it shows Macbeth pretending to love Duncan.

This is then explained to the reader.

Connective 'however' links us to the new impression. There is also more detail than before.

'But' signals a further idea, which is supported by the quotation by Macduff about Lady Macbeth's fainting.

'So' is used to introduce a summing up of the points made so far.

The impression we get of Macbeth here is of someone who **seems able to hide his feelings**, and is actually a very good ~~here and is a really great~~ actor ~~in this bit~~ because he is able to pretend that he is upset by the king's death. For example, when called upon to defend why he killed the guards he asks,

'Who could refrain that had a heart to love?'

He is saying that his anger and love for Duncan made him act in haste and fury.

~~I do repent me of my fury~~
~~That I did kill them~~

However, this is not all. We already know Macbeth has killed Duncan, but now he is admitting he killed the grooms (whom we know to be innocent). ~~Macbeth says this about the servants he killed saying he's sorry for what he did.~~ He killed them so they couldn't be questioned. This gives an ~~is pretty~~ evil impression.

But perhaps he is not ~~can't be~~ that good an actor because Lady Macbeth has to pretend to faint ~~to stop people looking at him.~~ while he explains himself to Macduff. In fact, Macduff has to suddenly stop and call out:

'Look to the lady.'

So the impression we get is of someone who is trying to cover up what he's done but someone who is ~~so he's~~ not really in control. ~~is he?~~

Marker's comment

I see the difference – detail, evidence, explanation, style!

This response now:
● links the points made effectively
● develops ideas more fully
● uses relevant quotations and explains what they mean
● keeps the focus on the question – the **impressions** we get of Macbeth
● reads fluently, with an appropriate style and tone (nothing too chatty or informal).

Overall level: **(high) level 6/borderline level 7**, on the evidence of this section.

Gaining the highest level

*do **brilliantly** !*

In order to get the highest marks possible, however, your answer needs to have **something special**. You need to mix two very important things:

- **insight** – looking beyond the obvious and really seeing into the heart of the play and its characters
- **imaginative and detailed expression of your ideas** – you need to write your ideas down in a way that will appeal to the Test marker.

Paragraph structure

Here is one example of how one small part of the Macbeth answer might be written:

What happens

The student states what happens clearly and concisely. There is no re-telling of the story.

Quotation

Note how well the quotation is *woven into* the point made – the expression is excellent.

> As Macbeth confesses to killing the guards and then gives his reasons for doing so, is it possible that two voices are speaking to us? One voice comes from Macbeth's dark side — pretending to be outraged by Duncan's 'silver skin laced with his golden blood'; the other is the voice of the man Macbeth might have been — his guilty voice, unable to believe what he himself has done. Perhaps this is the impression he gives to Macduff and the others, and this is why Lady Macbeth has to feign illness to draw attention from him.

Insight/suggestion

This insight into Macbeth's 'two voices' comes from the student knowing the play very well – from having seen Macbeth's guilty feelings and doubts earlier.

Explanation and development

Finally, the points are linked to new information.

QUICK CHECK

Improve the extract below from a level 5/6 answer.

You will need to **express** the ideas better; and **show insight** into **why** Macbeth might say what he says. Use an actual quotation. (This comes from Macbeth's speech before Malcolm and Donaldbain enter in Act 2 Scene 3.)

> When Macbeth finds out the King is dead he appears dead surprised and says he wanted to die an hour earlier and that everything worthwhile in life such as respect is gone. But we know he's faking it. Or is he?

This section contains:

- **two practice questions** on the set scenes for Macbeth (see pages 81 and 92)
- mark schemes for you to assess your own work and get a good idea of the **level requirements** (see pages 86 and 97)
- **sample answers** at different levels (see pages 87–91 and 98–102) with comments to help you improve your level.

Before turning to the Test questions, **read the information on this page carefully**.

Some important points

The set scenes from *Macbeth* for the 2005 Shakespeare Paper are as follows:

Act 3 Scene 1 (line 75 to the end of the scene):
'Was it not yesterday we spoke together?'
　　to
'If it find heaven, must find it out tonight.'
　　and

Act 3 Scene 2 (whole scene):
'Is Banquo gone from court?'
　　to
'So prithee, go with me.'
　　and

Act 3 Scene 4 (whole scene):
'You know your own degrees, sit down;'
　　to
'We are yet but young in deed.'

Remember

- Respond to the **question that has been set**, using the **key words from the question**.
- Write **clearly** using **whole sentences** and **paragraphs**.
- **Support** your points with **evidence** and **quotations**.
- **Link your ideas together** using **connectives**.
- **Check your writing** to see it is **clear** and **makes sense**.

- You will **not be given all** these scenes in the actual Test.
- You will be given **one question about shorter extracts** from **two of the scenes**.

The practice questions that follow are just two **possible** questions that could be asked, so do not think that you can learn the answers word for word for the Test or you will get a nasty shock! Therefore, it is important you revise all the set scenes mentioned above so that you don't get caught out.

Now **read question 1** and the extracts from the set scenes (on pages 82–85). Read the question carefully and remember to **plan your answer before you start to write**.

It is a good idea to **time yourself** when you revise like this – **you will only have 45 minutes in the Test!**

Yes, **read** the instructions first... That way I am sure I know what to do!

You should spend about 45 minutes on this question.

Macbeth

Act 3 Scene 2, line 8 to the end of the scene
Act 3 Scene 4, line 83 to the end of the scene

**How does Shakespeare use language to
convey Macbeth's emotions and behaviour
in these two scenes?**

Macbeth

Act 3 Scene 2, line 8 to the end of the scene

> In this scene Lady Macbeth and Macbeth discuss the threats to them and how to behave during the banquet at their palace.

A room in Macbeth's palace

Enter MACBETH

LADY MACBETH	How now, my lord, why do you keep alone	
	Of sorriest fancies your companions making,	
	Using those thoughts which should indeed have died	10
	With them they think on? Things without all remedy	
	Should be without regard; what's done, is done.	
MACBETH	We have scorched the snake, not killed it;	
	She'll close, and be herself, whilst our poor malice	
	Remains in danger of her former tooth.	15
	But let the frame of things disjoint, both the worlds suffer,	
	Ere we will eat our meal in fear and sleep	
	In the affliction of these terrible dreams	
	That shake us nightly. Better be with the dead	
	Whom we, to gain our peace, have sent to peace,	20
	Than on the torture of the mind to lie	
	In restless ecstasy. Duncan is in his grave.	
	After life's fitful fever, he sleeps well;	
	Treason has done his worst; nor steel nor poison,	
	Malice domestic, foreign levy, nothing	25
	Can touch him further.	
LADY MACBETH	Come on. Gentle my lord,	
	Sleek o'er your rugged looks, be bright and jovial	
	Among your guests tonight.	
MACBETH	So shall I, love,	
	And so I pray be you. Let your remembrance	30
	Apply to Banquo, present him eminence	
	Both with eye and tongue; unsafe the while, that we	
	Must lave our honours in these flattering streams	
	And make our faces vizards to our hearts,	
	Disguising what they are.	
LADY MACBETH	You must leave this.	35

| MACBETH | O, full of scorpions is my mind, dear wife! |
| | Thou know'st that Banquo and his Fleance lives. |

| LADY MACBETH | But in them Nature's copy's not eterne. |

MACBETH	There's comfort yet, they are assailable;
	Then be thou jocund: ere the bat hath flown	40
	His cloistered flight, ere to black Hecate's summons
	The shard-borne beetle with his drowsy hums
	Hath rung night's yawning peal, there shall be done
	A deed of dreadful note.

| LADY MACBETH | What's to be done? |

MACBETH	Be innocent of the knowledge, dearest chuck,	45
	Till thou applaud the deed. Come, seeling night,
	Scarf up the tender eye of pitiful day
	And with thy bloody and invisible hand
	Cancel and tear to pieces that great bond
	Which keeps me pale. Light thickens,	50
	And the crow makes wing to th'rooky wood;
	Good things of day begin to droop and drowse,
	Whiles night's black agents to their preys do rouse.
	Thou marvell'st at my words, but hold thee still;
	Things bad begun, make strong themselves by ill.	55
	So prithee, go with me.

Exeunt

Act 3 Scene 4, lines 83 to the end of the scene

In this extract, Macbeth is at a banquet in his own castle. He has just seen the ghost of Banquo, whose murder he himself organised.

| LADY MACBETH | My worthy lord, |
| | Your noble friends do lack you. |

MACBETH	I do forget –
	Do not muse at me, my most worthy friends.	85
	I have a strange infirmity which is nothing
	To those that know me. Come, love and health to all,
	Then I'll sit down. Give me some wine; fill full!

Enter GHOST [OF BANQUO]

I drink to th'general joy o'th'whole table,
And to our dear friend Banquo, whom we miss.   90
Would he were here! To all, and him we thirst,
And all to all.

LORDS   Our duties and the pledge.

MACBETH   Avaunt and quit my sight! Let the earth hide thee!
Thy bones are marrowless, thy blood is cold;
Thou hast no speculation in those eyes   95
Which thou dost glare with.

LADY MACBETH   Think of this, good peers,
But as a thing of custom. 'Tis no other,
Only it spoils the pleasure of the time.

MACBETH   What man dare, I dare;
Approach thou like the rugged Russian bear,   100
The armed rhinoceros, or th'Hyrcan tiger,
Take any shape but that, and my firm nerves
Shall never tremble. Or be alive again,
And dare me to the desert with thy sword;
If trembling I inhabit then, protest me   105
The baby of a girl. Hence horrible shadow,
Unreal mock'ry hence.
                    Exit Ghost of Banquo
                    Why so, being gone,
I am a man again. – Pray you, sit still.

LADY MACBETH   You have displaced the mirth, broke the good meeting
With most admired disorder.

MACBETH   Can such things be,   110
And overcome us like a summer's cloud,
Without our special wonder? You make me strange
Even to the disposition that I owe,
When now I think you can behold such sights
And keep the natural ruby of your cheeks,   115
When mine is blanched with fear.

ROSS   What sights, my lord?

LADY MACBETH   I pray you speak not; he grows worse and worse.
Question enrages him. At once, good night.
Stand not upon the order of your going,
But go at once.

| LENNOX | Good night, and better health | 120 |
| | Attend his majesty. | |

LADY MACBETH   A kind good night to all.

Exeunt Lords and Attendants

MACBETH	It will have blood they say: blood will have blood.	
	Stones have been known to move and trees to speak.	
	Augures, and understood relations, have	
	By maggot-pies, and choughs, and rooks brought forth	125
	The secret'st man of blood. What is the night?	

LADY MACBETH   Almost at odds with morning, which is which.

| MACBETH | How sayst thou that Macduff denies his person |
| | At our great bidding? |

LADY MACBETH   Did you send to him, sir?

MACBETH	I hear it by the way, but I will send.	130
	There's not a one of them but in his house	
	I keep a servant feed. I will tomorrow –	
	And betimes I will - to the weïrd sisters.	
	More shall they speak. For now I am bent to know	
	By the worst means, the worst; for mine own good,	135
	All causes shall give way. I am in blood	
	Stepped in so far that should I wade no more,	
	Returning were as tedious as go o'er.	
	Strange things I have in head that will to hand,	
	Which must be acted ere they may be scanned	140

LADY MACBETH   You lack the season of all natures, sleep.

MACBETH	Come, we'll to sleep. My strange and self-abuse
	Is the initiate fear that wants hard use;
	We are yet but young in deed.

Exeunt

Level indicators for question 1

Now it is time to **check the level** of your own response to question 1 (see page 81) and to see how you may be able to improve your answer.

At the beginning of this section (page 80), you were advised to make sure that you **answer** the question set, **support** your points with **evidence** from the text and **check your writing** to see that it **makes sense**.

Use the table below to assess the level of your work. Look at the indicators against each level and decide where your answer best fits.

There are also sample answers provided (see pages 87–91). Each sample answer is at a different level. You will probably find it useful to compare these with your own answer to get the best idea of your level.

Level	Indicators
4	• Some simple ideas about Macbeth's feelings and behaviour, perhaps referring to his fear and anxiety, but little sense of how these emotions vary. • Some explanation of what is said, supported by some quotations. The quotations are not always relevant and are rather clumsily inserted into the answer. • No real attempt to draw ideas together. • More reference to the story/plot than to understanding how language conveys Macbeth's behaviour. • Poor style makes ideas seem un-linked and not thought through.
5	• Greater understanding of how the language influences the impression we get of Macbeth and how he feels. Points lack development sometimes. • References to Macbeth's state of mind, using adjectives (i.e. *tense*, *scared*) but still some slipping into re-telling of events without explanation. • Focus on some individual words and phrases but restricted mostly to comments on simile and metaphor. • Quotations and evidence used but often explained in a rather clumsy way. • Occasional irrelevant comments which go off the point. • Accurate and reasonably helpful style and structure, but not very fluent or well-linked ideas.
6	• Closer and more detailed examination of the language used in the two extracts, and what this tells us about Macbeth. Some reference to his varying emotions (from fear and anxiety to planning and control). • Clear understanding of the way the scenes use imagery (metaphor and simile) and what these tell us. • A much greater focus on individual words and phrases relating to Macbeth and what they tell us. • Some attempt to draw wider links and references together but not always successfully. • Answer is well-written in clear paragraphs with ideas fluently expressed.
7	• Clear development of all points made with focused analysis of Shakespeare's use of language and what this tells us about Macbeth. • A wider understanding of how the language echoes other themes and concerns at other stages in the play. • Comments go beyond just simile and metaphor, but also focus on verse, rhythm and couplets. Language structures may be referred to, such as powerful words, sounds, repetition and contrasts. • Quotations are wide and varied, and there is good knowledge of the play as a whole and the function played by these specific scenes within the play. • Answer shows insight and is fully developed with ideas explored in a fluent and coherent way. • Answer is individual, with a clear style and the student shows flair in both their analysis and use of language.

Sample answers to question 1

Student A

The comments on these sample answers are colour-coded to help you identify the weak and strong areas. When comments are **green** it means that the student has done something well, **amber** indicates that some **improvement is needed**, and **red** means that the student needs to look again and maybe go back to the drawing-board!

Quotation is used, but not really the right one to show **Macbeth's** frame of mind

Good style – new paragraph introduces new point.

Quotation is relevant and an explanation is given.

New paragraph needed.

Very little on the second scene and there is too much retelling of the story.

Shakespeare **uses lots of descriptions** in these scenes about Macbeth and Lady Macbeth. These tell us lots of things about them such as that **he's really worried about what he's done** and is guilty.

She says to him: **'What's done is done'** which means he can't go back and change things even if he wanted to.

There's a lot about fear in the first bit and how Macbeth **can't really eat anything because he's afraid** that he will be caught and done for the murder.

At the end of the scene there is a lot about the nightime because that is the time when murder is done. Macbeth says:

'Come, seeling night,
Scarf up the tender eye of pitiful day'

and this means that he wants night to come because he can get on with things like Banquo's murder.

At the beginning he also says: **'my mind is full of scorpions'. This is a good description because it tells us he has poisonous thoughts that stop him sleeping. The next scene is the banquet scene. In this scene** Macbeth sees the ghost of Banquo. Banquo was killed by three men and now the ghost has appeared. Macbeth says: 'Avaunt and quit my sight!' 'Quit' means 'leave' so **he wants the ghost to leave him in peace so we can see that nothing has changed.** He is still afraid and his wife has to make him behave or he'll say something stupid.

But at the end he is ok and he plans to kill Macduff.

Introduction is a bit vague.

Explanation is relevant but is a little lacking in detail.

New point does not add much and there is no supporting quotation.

New point introduced rather suddenly and not really linked to other ideas. Has it been quoted correctly?

Explanation about Macbeth's feelings but it is very undeveloped.

Marker's summary

- This response shows some awareness of how language can reveal Macbeth's state of mind to us. The section on the first extract is quite good, even if the ideas are undeveloped and are rarely linked to make wider points.
- The second extract is hardly touched on, though, and what is there is mostly a retelling of the story.
- Quotations and some explanations are included but there is insufficient comment on imagery and individual words and phrases.
- This would receive a **low level 4**.

Student B

Shakespeare uses lots of great language in these scenes to tell us how Macbeth feels and behaves. There are many good descriptions and ways of saying things that tell you exactly how he is feeling. You can just imagine you are there inside his mind.

In the first scene, Macbeth talks about how his enemies are like a 'snake'. This is a metaphor. Macbeth says:

'We have scorched the snake, not killed it'.

This means that they have killed Duncan but his sons have escaped, and people like Banquo can't be trusted so they are still in danger. This is a really good description because snakes are still dangerous if you don't completely kill them.

Actually, Macbeth is really tense about things as a result. He even says he would like to be in Duncan's shoes who is dead.

'Duncan is in his grave. After life's fitful fever he sleeps well.'

This is amazing. He killed Duncan! Now he wants to be like him. Dead. Later he says to Lady Macbeth, his wife,

'O, full of scorpions is my mind, dear wife!'

This is a great description because you can imagine a spiky scorpion in his head not letting him sleep and causing him pain. This is really good imagery.

At the end of the scene he goes on about the night time and the darkness. It's a really violent description and shows that Macbeth really is a murderous and unpleasant man. He says,

'Come seeling night,
Scarf up the tender eye of pitiful day
And with thy bloody and invisible hand
Cancel and tear to pieces that great bond
Which keeps me pale,'

This is all about how the night is like a killer and is attacking or blinding the daylight. It shows that even if Macbeth is afraid he is not going to stop doing bad things.

Starts by using words from the question but there is not a lot being said here.

Further explanation is correct but does it add anything?

New paragraph needed for new points.

New quotation to support point.

Further comments about language followed by an explanation.

Quotation supports the point made. The reference to 'metaphor' is correct but a bit clumsy.

A useful explanation of what is meant.

No need to praise Shakespeare – this is irrelevant!

Good attempt to explain the power of the description but could be expanded – **how** does it show what it shows. Does the student even understand?

New scene introduced; but it slips into re-telling of the story.

In the second scene Banquo has been killed and Macbeth is having a big feast. Everyone is there so it is his time to show off but he can't because he is thinking of other things. Then when the ghost appears it really shakes him;

'Let the earth hide thee!' he says.
He cannot believe what he just saw.
'Can such things be,
And overcome us like a summer cloud?'

Refers to the use of simile and tries to explain it but the point could be expanded.

This is a simile or comparison and is saying that bad things like ghosts can ruin your good moments.

Could do with a quotation here to support the point.

Further comments about Macbeth's behaviour in the scene.

Macbeth also says he is 'blanched with fear' which shows us he is really pale and white. By the end of the scene, though, Macbeth has sort of recovered. Shakespeare shows us how he feels by saying that

'I am in blood stepped is so far that should I wade no more,'
Returning were as tedious as go o'er.'

Important last quotation which is very relevant to Macbeth's state of mind.

This is a good description because it is like Macbeth is walking through water, but it is blood and he is halfway across so there's no point in turning back. He might as well continue killing.

Good attempt to conclude, if a little sudden.

So he has changed from the last scene where he is all anxious. Now he seems pretty sure what he needs to do.

Marker's summary

- This response gets to grips with how Shakespeare uses language and attempts to focus on the power of the imagery and what it tells us about Macbeth.

- On occasions, it slips into a 'praise Shakespeare' piece, which is not the purpose of the task, but the quotations are generally well-chosen, and there is a clear attempt to explain them and what they mean.

- Expression is a little clumsy in places ('This is a metaphor') and the student needs to be aware this is not about spotting similes/metaphors and ticking them off. There are other things that could be said about the language – use of verbs, extended metaphor, references to the 'agents of the night' etc but all in all this is a reasonably successful response.

- This would gain a **mid/high level 5** but with better expression and a little **more development** it would fall into the **level 6 bracket**.

Student C

Shakespeare uses language in several ways to show us Macbeth's emotions and behaviour. In the first scene Macbeth is concerned that although he has killed Duncan, there are those that suspect him and may cause him harm in the future. He uses the metaphor of a 'scorched' snake that has only been wounded and will live to fight another day as a metaphor for his situation. This reference to poisonous or dangerous creatures is repeated later in the scene when Macbeth says:

'O, full of scorpions is my mind, dear wife!' which sounds like the anguished cry of someone who cannot find peace. You can imagine him clutching his head on stage.

Another way Macbeth's feelings are described is when he talks about sleep. Sleep is mentioned lots of times in the play so it is obviously on Macbeth's mind, which is not surprising considering that he has committed murder. In this scene he talks about how it is 'better' to be with the dead who have been sent 'to peace'. He mentions that Duncan now 'sleeps well,' almost as if he envies the people he has murdered!

In the same scene, there are some particularly strong descriptions of night time made by Macbeth. He mentions things to do with the night — the 'bat', the 'shard-borne beetle' and later the 'crow' and 'th'rooky wood'. These are all 'black agents' of the night and through Macbeth's mention of them he is kind of associating himself with them. Therefore, although he can't sleep — he wants night to come because it is when he can commit murder. The scene ends with him hiding information from his wife — he reveals no more than that he is going to do a 'deed of dreadful note'. This is powerful because we know what Macbeth has planned, but Lady Macbeth doesn't.

The second scene is very different because Banquo has been murdered and you think that maybe Macbeth will now be a little more relaxed and feel safe. But when he sees the ghost of Banquo even though he tries to cover up his feelings he cannot:

'Avaunt and quit my sight! Let the earth hide thee! Thy bones are marrowless, thy blood is cold.'

Good introduction to the point.

Reference to the metaphor used is made simply and clearly.

Idea is well-linked to later references.

Nice touch to talk about Macbeth's behaviour/ actions.

Reasonable exploration of an idea, but where is it mentioned in the play? Give examples.

Further point and more development of ideas.

Interesting new point – is this really to do with language use, though?

Insight and clear explanation of new point focusing on specific words.

New scene introduced by new paragraph, fluently linked.

Explanation followed by relevant quotation.

These descriptions of the 'living-but-dead' Banquo really show how Macbeth is shaking. He cannot believe how real it is.

'Can such things be/And overcome us like a summer's cloud...?'

This simile links to other descriptions of day and night, light and darkness that have surfaced in the play. Macbeth then goes on to talk about the supernatural and seems almost to be talking in a witch-like spell — 'blood will have blood.'Stones have been known to move and trees to speak.'.

From this, and all his references to night and creatures of the night, it seems as if Macbeth is feeling and behaving like a devilish creature himself so that at the end of the scene it is not surprising when he uses the metaphor of being 'stepped in so far' in blood, like a river crossing, that he can't go back.

He ends his last long verse speech with a couplet — as if he has made up his mind and can't now change things:

'Strange things I have in head that will to hand
Which must be acted ere they may be scanned.'

New quotation further backs up the explanation.

Links ideas across the play though an example from elsewhere would help.

He cannot believe how real it is.

Develops explanation and shows insight.

This paragraph is all one sentence!

Good to end with a reference to verse and refer to the couplet and its purpose. But why is a couplet particularly appropriate?

Marker's summary

- A very successful response that covers a wide range of ways Shakespeare uses language to reveal Macbeth's character. What is good about this answer is that the student does not just stick to simile and metaphor. There is a comment on individual words and phrases, links to other parts of the play (though there could be more of this) and even reference to the couplet at the end of the speech and how this tells us something about Macbeth's feelings.

- The main weakness is missing out on some obvious links, e.g. Macbeth's speech about the 'seeling night' is a direct parallel with Lady Macbeth's 'Come you spirits,' speech in Act 1 Scene 5. By and large the expression is fluent and the points are linked, although there are some undeveloped points ('Sleep is mentioned lots of times in the play...' — When? How? Why?)

- This is very competent response and would gain a **high level 6/low level 7**.

QUESTION 2

You should spend about 45 minutes on this question.

Macbeth

Act 3 Scene 1, lines 77 to 125
Act 3 Scene 4, lines 15 to 75

**What different impressions do we get of
Macbeth in these two extracts?**

Macbeth

Act 3 Scene 1, lines 77 to 125

> **In this extract, Macbeth talks to two men about plans to murder Banquo.**

MACBETH	Well then, now have you considered of my speeches?
	Know, that it was he in the times past which held you so under
	fortune, which you thought had been our innocent self. This I
	made good to you in our last conference; passed in probation 80
	with you how you were borne in hand, how crossed; the instru-
	ments, who wrought with them, and all things else that might to
	half a soul and to a notion crazed say, 'Thus did Banquo.'
FIRST MURDERER	You made it known to us.
MACBETH	I did so, and went further, which is now our point of 85
	second meeting. Do you find your patience so predominant in
	your nature, that you can let this go? Are you so gospelled, to
	pray for this good man and for his issue, whose heavy hand
	hath bowed you to the grave and beggared yours forever?
FIRST MURDERER	We are men, my liege. 90
MACBETH	Ay, in the catalogue ye go for men,
	As hounds, and greyhounds, mongrels, spaniels, curs,
	Shoughs, water-rugs, and demi-wolves are clept
	All by the name of dogs. The valued file
	Distinguishes the swift, the slow, the subtle, 95
	The housekeeper, the hunter, every one
	According to the gift which bounteous nature
	Hath in him closed, whereby he does receive
	Particular addition from the bill
	That writes them all alike. And so of men. 100
	Now, if you have a station in the file
	Not i'th'worst rank of manhood, say't,
	And I will put that business in your bosoms,
	Whose execution takes your enemy off,
	Grapples you to the heart and love of us 105
	Who wear our health but sickly in his life,
	Which in his death were perfect.
SECOND MURDERER	I am one, my liege,
	Whom the vile blows and buffets of the world
	Hath so incensed that I am reckless what I do
	To spite the world.

2

FIRST MURDERER	And I another,	110
	So weary with disasters, tugged with fortune,	
	That I would set my life on any chance	
	To mend it or be rid on't.	

MACBETH	Both of you know
	Banquo was your enemy.

MURDERERS	True, my lord.

MACBETH	So is he mine, and in such bloody distance	115
	That every minute of his being thrusts	
	Against my near'st of life; and though I could	
	With barefaced power sweep him from my sight	
	And bid my will avouch it, yet I must not,	
	For certain friends that are both his and mine,	120
	Whose loves I may not drop, but wail his fall	
	Who I myself struck down. And thence it is	
	That I to your assistance do make love,	
	Masking the business from the common eye	
	For sundry weighty reasons.	

SECOND MURDERER	We shall, my lord,	125
	Perform what you command us.	

Act 3 Scene 4, lines 15 to 75

> **In this extract, Macbeth is about to host a banquet for the other Thanes (lords) but then the murderers arrive with news of Banquo.**

MACBETH	…Is he dispatched?	15

FIRST MURDERER	My lord, his throat is cut; that I did for him.

MACBETH	Thou art the best o'th'cut-throats,
	Yet he's good that did the like for Fleance;
	If thou didst it, thou art the nonpareil.

FIRST MURDERER	Most royal sir, Fleance is scaped.	20

MACBETH
Then comes my fit again: I had else been perfect;
Whole as the marble, founded as the rock,
As broad and general as the casing air:
But now I am cabined, cribbed, confined, bound in
To saucy doubts and fears. But Banquo's safe?   25

FIRST MURDERER
Ay, my good lord: safe in a ditch he bides,
With twenty trenchèd gashes on his head,
The least a death to nature.

MACBETH
                                   Thanks for that.
There the grown serpent lies; the worm that's fled
Hath nature that in time will venom breed,   30
No teeth for th'present. Get thee gone; tomorrow
We'll hear ourselves again.

Exit [First] Murderer

LADY MACBETH
                              My royal lord,
You do not give the cheer; the feast is sold
That is not often vouched while 'tis a-making
'Tis given with welcome. To feed were best at home: 35
From thence, the sauce to meat is ceremony,
Meeting were bare without it.

Enter the GHOST OF BANQUO *and sits in Macbeth's place*

MACBETH
                              Sweet remembrancer!
Now good digestion wait on appetite,
And health on both.

LENNOX
                              May't please your highness, sit.

MACBETH
Here had we now our country's honour roofed,   40
Were the graced person of our Banquo present,
Who may I rather challenge for unkindness
Than pity for mischance.

ROSS
                              His absence, sir,
Lays blame upon his promise. Please't your highness
To grace us with your royal company?   45

MACBETH
The table's full.

LENNOX
                              Here is a place reserved, sir.

MACBETH
Where?

LENNOX
Here, my good lord. What is't that moves your highness?

2

MACBETH	Which of you have done this?	
LORDS	What, my good lord?	
MACBETH	Thou canst not say I did it; never shake	50
	Thy gory locks at me!	
ROSS	Gentlemen, rise, his highness is not well.	

[Lady Macbeth joins the Lords]

LADY MACBETH — Sit, worthy friends. My lord is often thus,
And hath been from his youth. Pray you, keep seat.
The fit is momentary; upon a thought   55
He will again be well. If much you note him
You shall offend him and extend his passion.
Feed, and regard him not. *[To Macbeth]* Are you a man?

MACBETH — Ay, and a bold one, that dare look on that
Which might appal the devil.

LADY MACBETH —   O proper stuff!   60
This is the very painting of your fear;
This is the air-drawn dagger which you said
Led you to Duncan. O, these flaws and starts,
Impostors to true fear, would well become
A woman's story at a winter's fire   65
Authorised by her grandam. Shame itself!
Why do you make such faces? When all's done
You look but on a stool.

MACBETH — Prithee, see there! Behold, look, lo! How say you?
[To Ghost] Why, what care I? If thou canst nod, speak too.   70
If charnel houses and our graves must send
Those that we bury back, our monuments
Shall be the maws of kites.

[Exit Ghost of Banquo}

LADY MACBETH —   What, quite unmanned in folly?

MACBETH — If I stand here, I saw him.

Level indicators for question 2

Now it is time to **check the level** of your own response to sample question 2 (see page 92) and to see how you may be able to improve your answer.

There are also sample answers provided (see pages 98–102). Each sample answer is at a different level. You will probably find it useful to compare these with your own answer to get the best idea of your level.

Level	Indicators
4	• Some simple ideas about Macbeth but with little or no attempt to compare and contrast his feelings and behaviour in the two scenes. • Some explanation of what is said, supported by some quotations, but these are not always relevant, and are rather clumsily inserted into the answer. • No attempt to draw ideas together. • More reference to the story/plot than to Macbeth's character. • Poor style makes ideas seem un-linked and not thought through.
5	• Greater understanding of the different impressions we get of Macbeth and the differences in his behaviour and language. • Some points made lack development. • References to Macbeth's state of mind – using adjectives (i.e. *tense*, *scared*) but still some slipping into re-telling events without explanation. • Focus on some individual words and phrases but restricted mostly to comments on longer phrases or lines. • Quotations and evidence used but often explained in a rather clumsy way. • Occasional irrelevant comments which go off the point. • Accurate and reasonably helpful style and structure, but not very fluent or well-linked.
6	• Closer and more detailed examination of Macbeth in the two extracts and how the impressions we get vary according to his fears, anxieties, control etc. • Clear understanding of the way Macbeth responds to what happens to him and what he can/cannot control. • Much greater focus on individual words and phrases relating to Macbeth and what they tell us. • Some attempt to draw wider links and references together but not always successfully. • Answer is well-written in clear paragraphs with ideas fluently expressed.
7	• Detailed development of all points made, with focused analysis of Macbeth in these scenes, and their relation to the play as a whole. Likely to pick up on parallels with earlier scenes or ways of behaving. • A wider understanding of how these impressions echo other characteristics displayed by him at other times. • Clear focus on powerful words, images, and devices used (such as rhetorical questions in the speech with the Murderers) which convey his state of mind. • Quotations are wide and varied, and there is good knowledge of the play as a whole and the function played by the specific scenes within the play. • Answer shows insight and is fully-developed with ideas explored in a fluent and coherent way. • Evidence of original thinking and exploration of new ideas.

Sample answers to Question 2

Student A

As, with sample question 1, when a comment is **green** it means that the student has done something well, **amber** indicates that some **improvement is needed**, and **red** means that the student needs to look again and maybe go back to the drawing-board!

Starts by setting the scene – rather a waste of time.

In the first scene Macbeth is planning the murder of his old friend Banquo and Banquo's son Fleance. He is speaking to two Murderers and he is trying to persuade them to do the murder.

Uses an adjective to describe Macbeth but there is no quotation to support it.

Quotation is partly relevant, but not fully explained – what does this tell us about Macbeth?

Macbeth tells the men that Banquo is to blame for making them poor. He tells them this to make them kill Banquo. **This is clever** because if you are told to do something to someone you wouldn't do it without a reason. **So Macbeth shows he is clever.**

Does this need to be repeated?

But then he also insults the men. He calls them:

New paragraph needed – bad style.

'Ay in the catalogue ye go for men...' which sounds like he's saying you might be called 'men' but are you? I don't know why he does this, perhaps to make them angry. In the scene Macbeth says he can't just get rid of Banquo himself because lots of people like him so it needs to be done by someone else. This shows that Macbeth is really evil if he is even plotting to kill his old best friend.

New point about the impression we get of Macbeth.

Slips into retelling the story, but does add a point about Macbeth's state of mind.

In the second scene Macbeth thinks it is all sorted but then the murderers tell him that Fleance has escaped and Macbeth seems sort of mad and crazy.

Slang!

'Then comes my fit again.' A fit is like an attack of illness. Then when the Ghost comes in he is really scared senseless. 'never shake thy gory locks at me.' We realise he is just a coward really. He even says he's not to blame! 'Thou canst not say I did it.' This makes lady Macbeth really cross because she thinks he has bottled it and everyone will find out.

Suitable quotation. Followed by explanation, but not a detailed one.

Good new point made and quotation given to support it.

So Macbeth comes across as evil and clever to start with but he is just frightened at the end.

Attempt to sum up impressions but rather brief and undeveloped.

Marker's summary

- The first half of the answer contains ideas that are not clearly developed. Much of the answer does not focus enough on the impressions we get nor how these are conveyed. The writing jumps around a lot and as a result it is difficult to follow points through.

- The second half of this response is more successful than the first – there are a greater number of quotations, and even an attempt to contrast the impressions we get of Macbeth in both scenes.

- This response would gain a **low level 4**.

Student B

Introduction sets the scene and gets straight to the point.

Uses a word from the question and adjectives to describe the character but the comment is brief.

New point which is relevant, followed by comment.

New paragraph needed to move onto next scene.

Good insertion of quotations into the sentence, but no comment on the repetition of the sound 'c'.

Macbeth is very different in these two scenes. In the first he is pretty much in control — or he seems to be. He has obviously planned the murder of Banquo because he says:

'...have you considered of my speeches?'
which shows they've met before.

The impression given is of someone who is cool and clever — who is good at planning evil acts.
He is also clever because he is not going to do the murder himself. His reasons are:

'For certain friends that are both his and mine, Whose loves I may not drop.'

He is thinking like a mastermind, planning every move to make sure he keeps in power.

He is also very cunning in how he comes across to the murderers. He is really in control and even compares them to dogs, but he also questions their manhood:

'...if you have a station in the file
Not i'th'worst of manhood...'

This means — if you want to be seen by me as proper men not useless then do what I say. It's like he's challenging them and taunting them.

Another impression may be that he is quite scary. After all he does say he could use 'barefaced power' to get rid of Banquo. Maybe that would frighten them — and he has already said nasty things about them, and taunted them. In the banquet scene Macbeth seems different. When he finds out that Fleance has escaped he doesn't hide the fact that this worries him.

'Then comes my fit again.' He says he is 'cabbined, cribbed, confined...' This means he feels imprisoned, but soon he is planning more murders as he says he'll talk to the murderers again.

This gives the impression of someone who is desperate to finish things off.

Quotation supports point made but no expansion is made.

Quotation, followed by further explanations to take the point further.

Another new point but introduced a little abruptly with no link to what has been said before.

Good exploration and deeper thinking.

New points and evidence.

Then when the Ghost appears Macbeth seems to become even more crazy. He doesn't seem to care what he says even if it might give away the truth.

> 'Thou canst not say I did it; never shake
> Thy gory locks at me!'

But why does he say he didn't do it? Perhaps he fears God and wants to try to claim he is innocent? But he can't have it both ways, can he? This kind of sums him up. He doesn't know what to feel — one moment he is planning the murder, the next he is trying to pretend it didn't happen.

This of course makes Lady Macbeth really angry. She says 'This is the very painting of your fear' as if he has made it all up. It's just an illusion, so the impression we get is of a sort of madman.

Macbeth still thinks he is brave because he says he is a 'bold one' because he can look at things that would make the devil feel awful. But I don't think we get that impression. He seems pretty terrified to me.

This means we have had different impressions of him. In the first scene he was clever and calculating — and persuasive with the murderers. In the second he seems quite weak and baby-like and he can't face what he's done.

Relevant quotation but explanation is not very detailed or clear.

Use of first person – bad style.

Brief but appropriate conclusion – neatly sums things up but could be expanded.

Marker's summary

- This student makes many relevant points and uses appropriate quotations
- The main problem is that the response does not always hang together. There is too much jumping from one point to another. Several of the points are a little basic, e.g. the men are compared to 'dogs' but it is the different types of dogs that is important. Also, there is little mention of the rhetorical devices Macbeth uses to persuade the men.
- There is a lot of reference to the impressions given of Macbeth, which is good, and the response ends with a neat summary.
- This response would gain a **Level 5**.

Student C

Strong start – gives student's view straight away.

Macbeth is an enigma. Just when you think you have worked him out he does — or says — something that surprises you.

Slightly awkward style.

Take the first scene we are studying. In it Macbeth meets with two men who he persuades to murder Banquo for him. His reasons for not doing it himself?

'For certain friends that are both his
and mine,
Whose loves I may not drop...'

Supporting quotation.

Further development, use of keyword 'impression' and adjectives to describe character.

The obvious impression is that here we have a clever, calculating — political — man who needs to keep key people on board and can't afford to openly show what sort of person he is. But perhaps there's more to it than that. Perhaps Macbeth cannot face killing anyone personally? He was, after all, completely shaken up by the murder of Duncan — and later, when the Ghost of Banquo appears his shock and guilt are very apparent:

Student shows insight by exploring new ideas but could expand a little here.

'Thou canst not say I did it; never shake thy gory locks at me!'

Switches between the two scenes to make the point.

But back to Act 3 Scene 1. Whatever his reasons, Macbeth has planned carefully. He has met the murderers before as he asks them if they have 'considered' his previous speeches. We get the picture of a manipulating man who has set up the murderers (he has told them how Banquo was to blame for their misfortunes) and now he can introduce the 'point of second meeting' — the murder. He then uses many persuasive devices — for example rhetorical questions to influence the men. He says:

New point with evidence.

Refers to the language to support the point made.

'Do you find your patience so predominant in your nature, that you can let this go?'

He is taunting them, questioning their manhood and this is followed by references to them as 'dogs' in which he questions what rank or level they are. Clearly, Macbeth is no fool, and the impression given at this point is of someone who is pretty much in control.

Summary sentence sums up points made so far.

Link word
signals new
viewpoint.

Good description
of Macbeth's
state.

However, when we come to the banquet scene, the old Macbeth emerges. The old fears and doubts re-surface and we get the impression of someone who is trying desperately to survive – but is in torment. When he hears Banquo is dead, but not Fleance, he says how he is 'cabbined, cribbed, confined, bound in to saucy doubts and fears...' He seems to be like a man who can't escape the truth. Wherever he goes there will be the 'serpent' he hasn't quite killed (in an earlier scene he talked about having 'scorched the snake, not killed it...' and this is still the case now).

Supporting
quotations and
links to earlier
scenes.

Further links to
earlier scenes.

So, when the ghost appears his shock and wonder is hardly surprising. It is the same Macbeth who couldn't go back and place the daggers by Duncan's servants.

Now it is Lady Macbeth who taunts Macbeth, as he taunted the murderers..

> 'O these flaws and starts,
> Impostors to true fear, would well become
> A woman's story at a winter's fire...'

Supporting
quotation and
developed ideas.

Our impression now is of a man who cannot distinguish reality from illusion. The extract ends with him saying, 'If I stand here, I saw him...'

This Macbeth is a strange mix of the old and the new. He is shocked by what he has seen and the outcome of his clever planning, but we must not forget that he is soon acting alone, ordering new murders. This may even be the last time he feels real fear.

Good summary
statement.

Macbeth remains a clever man, but he cannot fight the future, or kill everyone who opposes him.

Conclusion a
little under-
developed.

Marker's summary

- This is a really fluent answer that signals its intentions from the start. Points are well-linked and there are references to the whole play, not just the two scenes. There is also evidence of independent thinking and real insight into what is going on.

- Sometimes there is a tendency to ask too many questions but by and large this is a well-argued and convincing response.

- This would be awarded a **level 7**.

QUICK CHECK Section 1

Unit 1 Brush up your Shakespeare

1. Because it is supposed to bring bad luck.
2. He was not a tyrant – he removed a weak ruler.
3. Elizabeth 1 and James 1
4. Raphael Holinshed – a historian
5. Possibly the Three Fates, from Greek mythology
6. He is credited with writing a book called *Demonology* which dealt with the supernatural.

Unit 2 The plot

Act 1
1. The Witches
2. A wounded Captain, and Ross
3. Thane of Cawdor
4. He will be father to future kings.
5. Malcolm
6. He should hide his feelings.
7. He says it seems 'pleasant'.
8. She welcomes Duncan, and speaks of the loyalty and respect due to him.
9. He speaks of his doubts, saying that Duncan is staying in his castle in 'double trust'.
10. She questions his manhood.

Act 2
1. Banquo
2. A dagger
3. Lady Macbeth
4. He cannot bear to think about what he has done.
5. Macduff
6. Macbeth kills the two servants.
7. Macduff
8. Macbeth pretends to be enraged by the murder of Duncan; Lady Macbeth (probably) pretends to faint.
9. It is like night-time – very dark.
10. He is going home to Fife. It suggests he does not support Macbeth.

Act 3
1. He is angry that Banquo's children will be kings one day, benefiting from the murders Macbeth has committed.
2. The Macbeths need to eliminate others to be completely safe.
3. She is concerned that Macbeth is still having difficulty hiding his feelings.
4. Fleance
5. Banquo's descendants can still be king, so the prophecy can still come true.
6. In Macbeth's chair
7. She says it is just an illness he has had since he was a youth.
8. Hecate
9. With the English king, in England
10. Macduff

Act 4
1. A child with a crown, holding a tree who says Macbeth cannot be harmed until Birnam Wood moves to Dunsinane (Macbeth's castle).
2. They all look like Banquo, and are his descendants.
3. Macduff has gone to England.
4. Ross
5. A 'messenger'
6. In King Edward's court, England
7. Malcolm says he would be more evil than Macbeth.
8. To test Macduff's loyalty.
9. He reveals the murder of Macduff's wife and children.
10. He should turn it to anger and revenge.

Act 5
1. She is trying to wash imaginary blood from her hands.
2. At the banquet
3. Donaldbain
4. He would not stay for any money or reward.
5. To hide how many there are of them.
6. Lady Macbeth
7. He reports that Birnam Wood is 'moving'. The witches prophesised that Macbeth would not be harmed until Birnam Wood moved to Dunsinane.
8. Young Siward – Siward's son
9. He was '*untimely ripped*' from his mother's stomach.
10. By her own hands, i.e. suicide

Unit 3 The characters

Macbeth
1. First mentioned by the Witches – so 'evil'
2. With the Witches, Act 1 Scene 3
3. He says Duncan is at his castle in 'double trust'.
4. Anxious and guilty
5. He no longer feels anything.
6. Banquo
7. His whole family were murdered on Macbeth's orders.
8. Siward's

Banquo
1. He helped to defeat the rebels.
2. With the Witches, Act 1 Scene 3
3. He says that what they say can be misleading.
4. He greets him, calls him 'noble'.
5. Because the Witches said Banquo's descendants would be kings, so if he kills Banquo and his son, he can stop this happening. Plus Banquo refuses to support him.
6. Fleance
7. As an apparition in Act 4 Scene 1

Lady Macbeth
1. Macbeth
2. Her feminine side
3. He looked like her own father.
4. We glimpse a weaker, softer side of her.
5. Blood
6. 'honoured hostess...fair and noble...'
7. In the last scene of the play (according to Malcolm).
8. The murder of Lady Macduff and her children.

Unit 4 Key themes

Ambition
1. Act 1 Scene 3
2. Malcolm
3. Mark Antony
4. In the letter Macbeth sends to her.
5. She would kill the child she was nursing.
6. She drugs the servants, takes the daggers back into the chamber and smears blood on them.

Order and chaos

1. Kings were considered to be chosen by God.
2. 'Fair is foul, and foul is fair'.
3. How he has destroyed sleep – the most natural thing.
4. He sees Banquo's ghost.

Appearance and reality

1. He fought with the rebels against Duncan's army.
2. 'worthiest cousin', a 'peerless kinsman'
3. He says how pleasant it is, yet this is where Duncan will be murdered.
4. Lady Macbeth
5. He appears to have been born 'naturally' but in fact was born by Caesarean section, which means Macduff fulfils the Witches prophecy which enables him to kill Macbeth.

Good and evil

1. He calls him 'gracious' and says his 'virtues will plead like angels...'.
2. Lady Macduff's children
3. He has experienced his father's murder and learnt not to trust by appearance.
4. Macduff
5. Lady Macbeth

The supernatural

1. Macbeth and Banquo – no one else
2. They cast spells, look into the future and give riddles.
3. To Duncan's bedchamber
4. Banquo's ghost
5. That the information they give is misleading.

Unit 5 Use of language

1. Any three from the following (or others from the Witches' speeches): poisoned entrails, sweltered venom, ravined salt-sea shark, finger of birth-strangled babe, fillet of fenny snake, eye of newt, toe of frog, lizard's leg.
2. (a)
3. (b): Duncan was stabbed, not strangled.
4. (c)
5. (a)
6. Scotland is described as follows: it weeps, bleeds, has a gash and wounds.

QUICK CHECK Section 2

Unit 1 Understanding the question

Skill area: character and motivation
Key words are in bold: **What different impressions** do **we** get of the **Witches** in these **two scenes**?

Unit 2 Finding and using evidence

How she behaves: Repeatedly going to her cupboard, writing upon a piece of paper, reading it, sealing it and locking it away before returning to bed (all in her sleep); she continuously rubs her hands as if she is washing.

What she says: 'Out damned spot!'; '...who would have thought the old man to have had so much blood in him?';
'Here's the smell of blood still; all the perfumes of Arabia will not sweeten this little hand';
'The Thane of Fife had a wife. Where is she / now? What, will these hands ne'er be clean?';
'I tell you again, Banquo's buried; he cannot / come out on's grave.'

What others do: The Doctor and the Gentlewoman watch her and listen to her.

What others say: Gentlewoman: 'She has spoke what she should not, I am sure of that.'
Doctor: 'Foul whisp'rings are abroad; unnatural deeds / Do breed unnatural troubles; infected minds / To their deaf pillows will discharge their secrets.'

Impressions: Lady Macbeth is a tormented woman and that she feels guilt about what she and her husband have done. There is also the impression that the others are aware from what she has revealed that she is guilty.

Unit 3 Paraphrasing, summarising and using quotations

A suitable answer would be: We can see that Lady Macbeth is suffering guilt from the way the doctor says her heart is sorely charged.

Unit 4 Structuring your answer

Possible adjectives:

	Act 1 Scene 7	Act 5 Scene 1
	murderous (2)	unstable (6)
	determined (3)	guilty (5)
	ambitious (1)	tormented (4)

Unit 5 Writing about two scenes

Opening paragraph: The two scenes provide opposing images. In the first, Lady Macbeth is ready to 'pour her spirits' into Macbeth's mind, and banish femininity. In the second, Lady Macduff, mother, protector, provides a complete contrast with the evil we have seen in Lady Macbeth.

Second paragraph: In this scene, evil rears its head in Lady Macbeth's words as she calls on 'murd'ring ministers' to take her blood for poison. Evil is also seen in the metaphor of the serpent, hiding under the 'innocent flower'.

Unit 6 What makes a top answer

Suggested improvement: While Macbeth may well be playing the part of the distraught subject as he reveals the King's death, his 'show' may equally be revealing an alternative truth. He claims that he'd have lived a 'blessed time' had he died before the King, implying therefore that dealing with the death of his King is too painful to bear and that he would sooner have died than find out. It could, however, be argued that he does indeed feel regret at the event – sad at the loss and sickened by his own actions. He may perhaps also be realising the crime he has committed against God.